Dearest Reba,

You are an inspiration
to us all!

Love & friendship,

Vicki B

robert jones
simple beauté

written with lisa bower and patricia young

ISBN 0-9717241-1-3

Hair & make-up: Robert Jones accompanied by Susie Jasper

Representation: Seaminx Artist Management   www.seaminx.com

Producer: Tiffany Mullen, Elaine Moock and Sunni Smyth

Fashion photography: Jeff Stephens

Fashion stylists: Barri Martin and Deborah Points, Chad Curry, Amy Simmonds (assistant stylist)

Still-life photography: Fernando Ceja and Cindy James

Still-life stylist: Linda Jantzen

Behind the scenes photography: Cindy James

Illustrations: Barbara Camp

Design and Art Direction: The Glassmoyer Group, Inc. New York City

Editor: Lisa Bower

www.simplebeaute.com

This book is dedicated to three very special people who have passed through my life, each of which I believe are now watching from above as guardian angels: my grandmother, Carolyn Walker Scoville (left), who was one of my first ideals of beauty; Bernardo Aldrete, no one ever believed in me more; and finally Diane Payne (right), a true inspiration.

8

10

embrace your own personal beauty---love who you are today and everyday.

— robert jones

truebeauty

This book is all about you---who you are, who you want to be and who you can be. I truly feel that every woman is beautiful. It is just a matter of recognizing your beauty and making it your focus.

I have long been convinced that beauty is not just about possessing a perfectly symmetrical face. Obviously it's marvelous to be blessed with exceptional features, but not all of the women I've made up in my many years as a professional makeup artist were flawless. Some of the most beautiful women I have ever seen or worked with are beautiful because of who they are and what comes from within. Beauty comes from the expression and character in your face---not just it's symmetry. It doesn't matter if you are short or tall, heavy or thin, or if your features aren't those of a fashion model or famous actress. Your beauty comes from self-awareness, self-confidence and your own magnetic personality. Actually, I feel that self-confidence is the most important element of true beauty.

My goal in writing this book is to help you bring out that beauty from within by increasing your self-confidence about your outward appearance. I want to demystify the art of makeup and help you understand how to use it as a tool to better appreciate who you are. Some women think makeup is far too difficult to master, but it's simple when you break it down. It's merely a matter of using the right products, good tools and the correct techniques.

"First and most importantly every woman needs to remember she is beautiful."

First and most importantly let me say that every woman needs to remember she is beautiful. By identifying your most striking features and accentuating them, we can make you look and feel more beautiful. Certainly one of the reasons I love being a makeup artist is the joy it gives me when I see how my work can change the way you feel about yourself. No matter what your age, if you are beautifully made up with bright eyes and a healthy glow, you will exude an aura of confidence that will draw people to you.

Modern makeup should be simple and natural so it's the face we notice not the makeup. I feel that cosmetics are to enhance the features God gave you, not to change them. I'm not suggesting natural makeup means walking around all day looking washed out. By simple and natural, I mean your makeup palette should be suited to your complexion and should change with each season to compliment the change in your skin's natural tone. Sometimes I'll notice a woman who obviously has made an effort with her makeup but has chosen a foundation color that's all wrong for her skintone, or she's wearing a lip color that's far too dark or vivid for her. The concept that "less is more" definitely holds true for makeup.

Makeup is meant to be beautiful, and beautiful makeup is all about the colors you use and where you place them--- never about how much you put on. I also think that it is important to remember that the face is not flat. It's not one-dimensional therefore don't paint it that way. Makeup should be used to artfully sculpt and accentuate your best features--- that is the very essence and purpose of wearing makeup.

Keep in mind that there are very few hard-and-fast rules in makeup and beauty. Beauty is in the eye of the beholder. And since beauty is subjective, everything discussed in this book reflects my own personal views. Each professional makeup artist has his or her own style, as do each of you. Mine has been described by many as the 'Glamorous-Girl-Next-Door'---I guess because I think all women should look beautiful but be approachable, and a little glamour never hurts. I want to help you discover your own personal style. Whatever the season or event, beautiful makeup will boost your self-confidence, which in turn will make you feel good about yourself, which will translate into true beauty. So read on---experiment with your makeup---have fun with it, and together we'll discover a more self-confident and beautiful you.

15

"Makeup is meant to be beautiful, and beautiful makeup is all about the colors you use and where you place them--- never about how much you put on."

2
thewords

Mastering the art of makeup application begins with knowing some of the basic terms. As you read through the next couple of pages, you'll find the definitions for some of the most commonly used words in the makeup business. Get to know and understand them and you'll soon be talking like a makeup pro.

matte satin

dewy

sheer eyeliner

pearlescent

gloss

aque powder

metallic

concealer

BLUSH: is for adding a wonderfully warm glow to the face. It can brighten the dullest of skin. If your cheeks are naturally rosy you might skip the blush and leave the glow up to Mother Nature.

CONCEALER: is a miracle product that hides everything your foundation doesn't. It makes broken capillaries, undereye circles, age spots and any skin discolorations disappear.

CONTOUR: the opposite of highlight. Everything that we contour we push away from the eye to make it appear less visible. A "contour" shade is usually a darker shade that  gives your features more depth and definition by contrasting against the lighter shades used on your face and around the eyes. Contouring is also the last step in the three-color layering technique for the eyes.

DEWY: often refers to foundation finishes that create a fresh and glowing look with a slight sheen.

EYELINER: for defining and "bringing out" the eyes, though it is not always necessary. Eye shadow: is either applied lightly as a gentle color wash or as a more dramatic layering of color and texture to enhance and add shape to the eyes.

FOUNDATION: is a miracle product that evens out your complexion and covers all imperfections. Your foundation's tone depends entirely on your skin. If your skin is looking radiant and beautiful without help, then by all means skip the foundation and go to a light dusting of powder. However, if you do need foundation, it comes in a variety of texture finishes such as matte, satin and dewy. If you have oily or blemished skin,

choose matte. If your skin is normal or dry, you can choose from any of the finishes.

FROST: is about maximum sparkle and super-shine. It is also sometimes referred to as iridescent. It is a fun, sexy look and works best on young skin because on more mature skin, 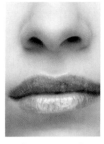 it can draw attention to the fine lines. The term is usually used in reference to eye shadows and lip color.

GLOSS: is a super high-shine lip color. It can add a punch of color but does not stay on as long as lipstick.

HIGHLIGHT: is the opposite of contour. Everything we highlight comes toward the eye and helps draw attention to a specific area or feature. A highlight shade is usually a lighter shade used on the face and the eyes. Highlighting is the first step in the three-color layering technique for the eyes.

LIP COLOR: is the quickest way to set the mood of your overall look. You can go all out and define your lips with color, or you can smear a clear gloss or healing lip balm for that pared-down, natural look.

LUMINESCENCE: describes a foundation with light-reflecting qualities that creates a glowing, refined look. The light-reflecting properties contain specially shaped particles that bounce light away from surface lines and wrinkles to create a more youthful look.

MASCARA: gives you those full, long, thick and dark lashes you've always wanted. If I've just described your natural lashes, an eyelash curler may be all it takes to spotlight your baby  blues, browns, greys, or greens. (If marooned on a desert island, mascara would be the number one makeup product most women would like to have with them.)

MATTE: is used to describe lipsticks, eye shadows, foundations, powders and blushes that have absolutely no shine and appear flat. Matte lipsticks tend to be drier, but they stay on much longer. Matte foundations are excellent on shiny and oily skins and are best for skins with imperfections. There are also matte products such as powders and crèmes that will help fight oils during the day.

METALLIC: describes lipsticks, eye shadows and eye pencils that have a shiny, metal finish. It's a look that is fantastic on ebony or darker skin but too harsh for lighter or more mature skin.

MIDTONE: a neutral, natural eye color that you sweep across the eyelids to help define and shape the eyes. The midtone shade should be a natural extension of your complexion and is the second step in the three-color layering technique for the eyes.

OPAQUE: is a finish that provides absolute coverage, allowing nothing to show through.

POROSITY: the skin's ability to hold moisture. Moisturizer can "even out" the porosity of your skin and help your foundation, primer or concealer go on more smoothly.

POWDER: is for setting foundation. It gives your face a smooth finish and keeps shine under control.

SATIN: refers to a formulation that's neither as flat as matte nor as shiny as shimmer. A "soft satin finish" is often used to describe foundations and liquid cosmetics that give a soft, smooth finish to the skin. Satin products have a sheen to them but are not shiny. Satin eye shadows are particularly good for mature skin because they glide on smoothly and add a soft sheen to the skin.

SHEER: is a thinner and more transparent finish that gives the skin a glow. It usually contains silicone that allows makeup to glide on easily. The product clings less and

covers more smoothly without being opaque. Sheer products seem to disappear into the skin, giving it a soft, more natural appearance. Sheer foundation is fabulous for mature women since it helps their skin appear brighter and less lined. And it's perfect for younger skin tones that need to be evened out.

STIPPLING: a blending technique used for concealers and foundations. It's especially effective for blending out the edges of concealers. Stippling is also a great way to carefully apply one product over another. Just place some product, such as foundation, on your fingertips and apply in a gentle patting motion so as not to disturb or erase the product you've already applied underneath, such as concealer.

TEXTURE: is the finish a product gives you – the way it appears or your skin. For example, a blush can have a creamy or a powdery texture. Foundation can have a dewy,

creamy, sheer, matte or satin texture. Lipsticks can be glossy, matte or sheer. It's always wise to match your textures – powder on powder, crème on crème.

product knowledge

With so many products out there, it sometimes seems hard to know which one is right for you. Well, never fear. Together we'll talk about the various makeup products, their forms and what makes them unique, and how to use each. Aren't you feeling more confident already?

foundation

is your most important makeup investment. It can make your skin appear flawless, natural and give it a healthy glow. It can cover imperfections, blemishes and smooth out uneven skin tones. Wearing it correctly can do more for your appearance than practically any other makeup product. It can also be one of the most difficult to choose correctly.

When making your foundation choice, there are two things to consider. The first is to match your skin tone and depth so that your foundation looks natural. Secondly, it's important to match your skin type with the correct foundation formula. For example, if you have oily skin, sometimes the oils from your skin can mix with the product and make your foundation appear blotchy and uneven. Wearing the correct foundation formula for your skin type can help your foundation stay on longer.

My advice? Spend generously on your foundation. The cost of cosmetics from one company to another is not only because of the packaging but also because of the ingredients. The purer the ingredients, the more expensive a product will be. Higher priced foundations usually contain a higher quality of pigments which last longer on your skin and appear much more flattering. Cheaper foundations contain fewer and inferior pigments that usually don't wear as long. If you want to treat yourself, splurge on the best foundation you can afford to buy. Foundation and powder are the bases of your look and therefore, the most important. Save your pennies on less expensive color products so you can afford to play around and have fun with color.

Thanks to modern technology, we have many advanced foundations to work with that can appear almost invisible. You can choose from a variety of textures and formulas that will give you different types of coverages and finishes. A product's consistency and the way it actually goes onto the skin is the key to even, flawless coverage. The real goal for your foundation is for it to look as if you're not wearing any at all. You simply give the illusion of having healthy, beautiful skin.

foundation generally comes packaged in eight different forms:

STICK foundation is essentially a neatly packaged crème-foundation and concealer in one. Best for normal to dry skin, it is a good option for women who want more coverage. It offers ideal, maximum coverage for imperfections as well as covering ruddy and uneven skin tones. Stick foundation will give you quick coverage, but it can look a little heavy on clear skin where a lot of coverage is not needed.

LIQUID foundation is the most readily found and is suited to most---if not all---skin types. It is available from oil-free formulas all the way to moisturizing formulas and gives varying degrees of sheer-to-medium coverage depending on the brand and the formula. You can purchase liquid foundation in a bottle or a tube. When applied, it gives you more coverage than a tinted moisturizer but less than a crème foundation.

CRÈME foundation is smooth and milky and is specifically formulated for drier complexions. It gives the skin a natural finish while offering the highest coverage. I find it to be the most versatile because even though it tends to be of a thicker and heavier consistency it can be made sheerer simply by applying it with a damp sponge. Also, because of its great coverage, it can even be used as a concealer if you don't have severe under-eye circles. Crème foundation is great for dry skin; however, if you have dry flaky skin, beware, because it can look "cakey" and the result can be slightly dull and heavy-looking.

MOUSSE foundation is actually a crème foundation that has a whipped consistency. It generally comes in a jar rather than a compact, and it is usually lighter and sheerer than its compact counterpart. It evens out the skin tone without appearing heavy. I use mousse-textured formulas a lot because they seem to sink into the skin rather than sit on top of it. They give great coverage that appears very natural. They are fabulous on mature skin because they do not collect in fine lines like heavier crème formulas.

TINTED moisturizer is actually a moisturizer with a little color added. It's the sheerest of all the foundations, and it's perfect for use during the summer months when you feel like wearing next to nothing. It evens out the skin tone while providing minimal coverage.

CRÈME-to-POWDER foundation is quick and simple. It has a creamy texture that dries to a powder finish, so usually no additional dusting of powder is needed to set it. These formulas are kinder to oily skin than their crème counterparts because the powder helps cut down on excess shine.

POWDER COMPACT is a dual-finish powder foundation that gives a quick and convenient sheer-to-medium coverage. It is simply a pressed powder that can be used wet or dry. Used dry, it goes on like a pressed powder but gives you slightly more coverage. I find that it's perfect for young girls because it's low in oils and doesn't clog pores, and so there's little risk of pimples appearing without warning. And it's great for touch-ups when you're on the go. Applied with a brush, it gives you sheer coverage. Applied with a sponge, it gives you more coverage. Applied wet with a damp sponge, t gives you even more complete coverage, like most other liquid and crème foundations.

PIGMENTED MINERAL POWDER is simply a loose powder that adheres to the skin, providing medium to full coverage. In addition to giving you coverage it also contains vitamins and minerals to help treat the skin. It works much like a dual-finish powder foundation and is simple to apply, with a brush or a sponge.

concealer

comes in various formulations and textures. Different textures of concealers are used on different problem areas, so it's important to match the texture with the problem area. For example, a concealer used to cover under-eye areas should always be moist and creamy, whereas a concealer designed to cover breakouts or broken capillaries should be much drier in texture so it will adhere better and last longer.

SOLID CREAM STICK concealers give full coverage but are not always the easiest to blend. They are used primarily for hiding some of the more prominent blemishes and skin discoloration. They can also be used to minimize under-eye circles, but if you're going to use this texture make sure the consistency is creamy enough to blend well so as not to accentuate fine lines. Since the most delicate skin is under the eyes, using a hard-to-blend stick concealer can actually make the circles look far worse by drawing attention to them.

POT CONCEALER provides similar coverage to stick, but it is usually formulated with more moisturizing ingredients and is not quite as thick---much better for underneath the eyes. This is the concealer that's probably the most commonly used by professionals because of the great coverage it gives. Although usually creamy, it is also available in drier, oil-free formulas that are used to cover discoloration on the rest of the face.

TUBE CONCEALER has a creamier texture that's lighter and less likely to collect in fine lines, making it great for mature skin. It's also one of the most versatile forms of concealer. It provides terrific coverage and can be mixed with moisturizer or foundation to create a much sheerer product. It's also perfect to use under the eyes because it's one of the easiest to blend.

WAND CONCEALERS offer the lightest texture and are excellent for evenly smoothing skin tones. If the proper shade is used, you may apply it without a foundation because it will blend easily into bare skin. Wand concealers provide a quicker, slightly denser coverage than liquid foundation, and they're absolutely fabulous for a fast repair. Some dry to a powder-finish that's great for covering facial blemishes because the powder clings, enabling it to be longer wearing.

PENCIL CONCEALERS effectively cover tiny imperfections such as broken capillaries, blemishes and other tiny flaws. You simply draw it on. With an exact color-match they can be pinpointed without blending. Pencil concealers are also terrific for fixing lip lines.

OIL-FREE COMPACT CONCEALER formulations are best used on the face to hide pimples and spots. They are usually of a longer-wearing, drier texture that won't irritate breakouts. Because of their wearability they are also effective for covering age-spots and hyper-pigmentation.

HIGHLIGHT REFLECTING products thankfully are now available. They help to hide flaws but don't actually cover. Instead they have light-reflecting properties that refract light to help minimize shadowed areas. In other words they highlight (bring out) recessed areas such as the dark shadows created by bags and wrinkles. You simply apply it to the shadowed area, and it brightens it, making it appear less distinct. You should apply them sparingly. Too often they are confused with concealers, which they most definitely are not!

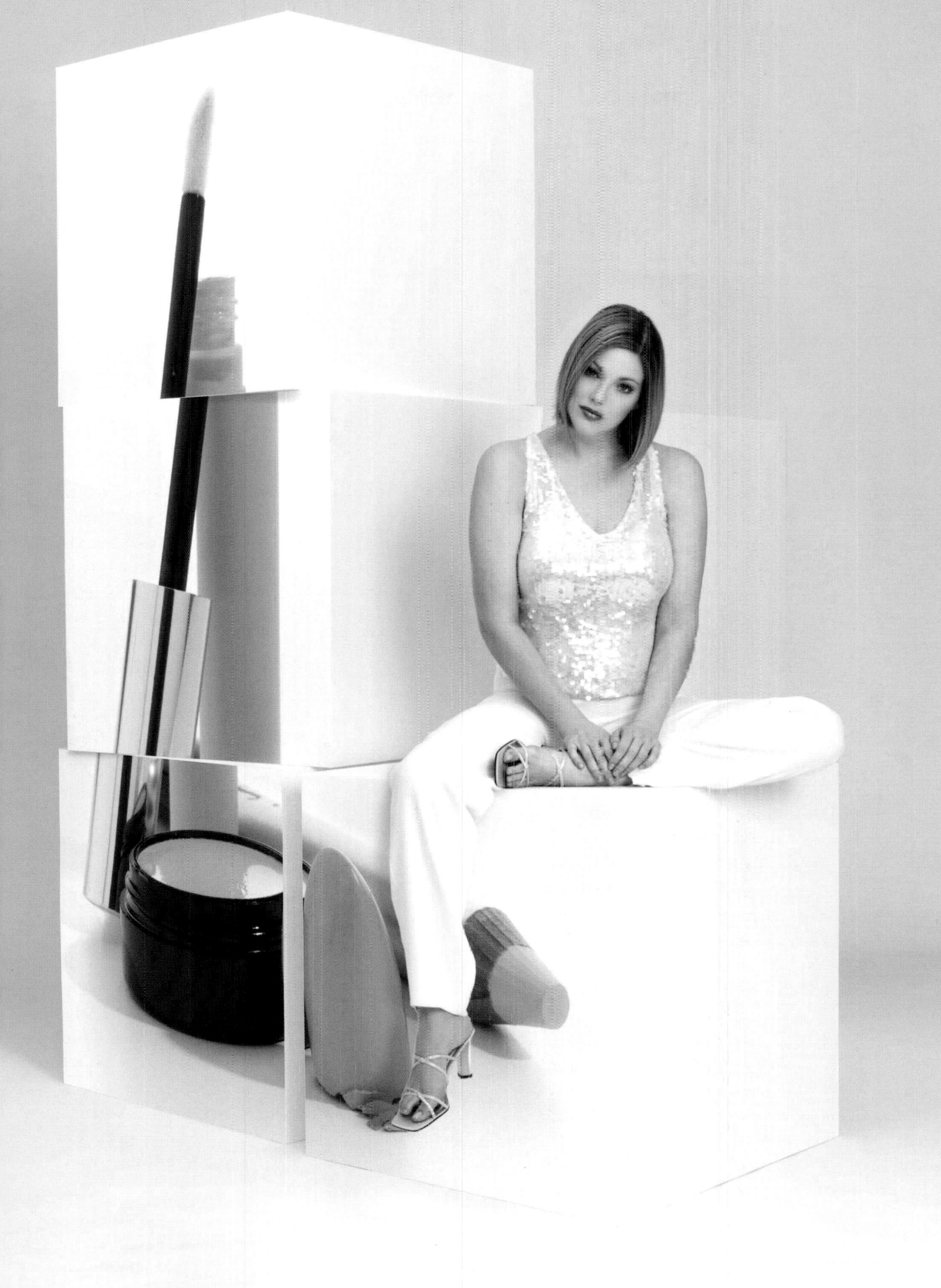

powder

Your makeup won't last the day without a little staying power from powder. It helps absorb the skin's natural oils to help control shine throughout the day. And it's the finishing step that helps your skin appear smooth and natural. You can even brush it on over a clean, moisturized face for a fresh, no-makeup look.

Most face powder is made from two bases – cornstarch and talcum. It basically comes in two forms, loose and pressed. Use a loose powder to set your makeup. It works the best and lasts the longest. Loose powder contains more oil absorbers than pressed, so it is the best choice for oily skin. Of course, if you travel, pressed powder is far more convenient to take along with you. Powder is an absolute must for oily skin. It absorbs extra oil from the skin and can be reapplied throughout the day. The finer a powder is milled, the higher the quality, so the less likely it is to cake on the skin. Finer-milled powders will feel more like velvet, whereas less-milled powders feel more gritty.

eyebrow

color is available in four formulas.

PENCIL is the most precise and common way to define the brows. It usually has a slightly more waxy consistency than other makeup pencils to help it adhere better to the brows and last longer. If you prefer a brow pencil, make sure it is sharpened because the sharper the point, the better the application.

POWDER brow color is a matte, no-shimmer powder with a very high pigment content. It is usually applied with a brush and can be used to set brow crèmes and pencils to help them last longer. Powder provides the most natural look when filling in your brows.

CRÈME is the most dramatic looking and looks the least natural. It is a matte crème that is applied with a brush, and it's best to set it with powder so it will last. It gives you the most opaque coverage, which is sometimes needed.

BROW GEL is basically a hair gel for the brows. It's great for unruly eyebrows because it helps keep the brows in place. Brow gels are available in tinted or clear formulas.

Tip: Be careful the eyebrow pencil you choose is not too waxy or it will be hard to apply evenly without looking harsh or fake.

mascara

generally comes in three formulas.

THICKENING mascara coats each individual lash from root to tip with particles that add bulk to the lashes and help them to look thick and full.

LENGTHENING mascara contains plastic polymers that cling just to the tips of the lashes, making them appear longer.

DEFINING mascara coats each individual lash, keeping them separated and defined. Defining mascara usually appears the most natural.

Most mascara is also available in a waterproof formula. However, unless you're susceptible to allergies that make your eyes water, I really don't recommend waterproof mascara because it's harder to remove and can be damaging to delicate lashes. Also, women with sensitive eyes might want to stay away from waterproof because it is the most irritating of all formulas.

Most women don't realize that the mascara wand is just as important to the finished result of your lashes as the mascara formula.

There are four basic brush shapes.

-- A crescent-shaped wand that helps curl the lashes up as you apply your mascara.

-- A fat, bristly wand that helps to thicken by coating each and every lash.

-- A wand that looks much like a screw, that either has very short bristles or none whatsoever. It allows you to define your lashes by painting each one right down to the root.

-- A double-tapered wand is a wand with smaller bristles at each end, tapering to fatter ones in the center. It works very nicely to define each thin, sparse lash while adding a little bulk.

It's always better to apply two thin coats of mascara rather than one thick, "clumpy" coat. I personally prefer thick, voluminous-looking lashes. I think they help define the eyes and they look so much more glamorous than thin, spidery-looking lashes.

eyeliner

comes in four basic formulas.

LIQUID eyeliner is a colored liquid that is applied with a fine-tip brush. Liquid stays on the longest and looks the most dramatic. You can also find it in felt-tip pens or with a pointed, sponge-tip applicator. Liquid liner is a good choice to use with strip false eyelashes because it successfully conceals the band of the lash. Liquid eyeliner should only be applied along the top lashline, never along the bottom lashline, because it looks too harsh and unnatural.

CAKE eyeliner is a pressed powder-like product that is applied with a damp brush. It will give you a similar effect to liquid eyeliner, but it's much easier to control.

CRÈME eyeliner is usually packaged in a pot and is applied using a damp brush. It will also give you a similar effect to liquid eyeliner. The fact that it dries much quicker makes it much easier to use without smearing it all over the place.

PENCIL is the most commonly used eyeliner simply because it's the easiest to control. There are many pencil textures available. Some are drier and harder and some are creamier and glide on effortlessly. In the past, many women felt the need to soften their hard, dry pencils using a lighter or a match. Thankfully, most pencils now contain silicone that enables them to glide on smoothly and makes them easy to smudge and blend. The best choice is a pencil with just enough silicone to glide on easily, but not so much that it smears or travels. Make sure your pencil is at least water-resistant so it will stay put and not smudge.

eyeshadow

comes in various textures and finishes.

TEXTURE:

POWDER SHADOWS come either loose or pressed. Both formulas vary from matte to shimmer and from iridescent to frosty. They are the most popular and the easiest to use because they blend so well. In most makeup lines, they offer the largest color choices in this texture.

CRÈMES are available in matte and shimmer. They are great for a wash of color across the whole lid. Some crème eyeshadows dry to a powder finish. You can also mix crème and powder eyeshadows together to increase the intensity of the shade.

LIQUID usually comes in a shiny, metallic finish and it's actually the hardest to use. Since it doesn't blend easily you must be more precise, so it's best when applied with a brush. Liquid is usually used either as an eyeliner or applied close to the lashline for color intensity.

PENCIL shadows are useful for around the eye because they are sharpened to a point and can be applied with such precision. When you've finished, you can simply smudge the line with your finger, a sponge-tip applicator or a brush to create the effect you want.

Tip: For a more intense color, try using both powder and crème shadows together.

Tip: Remember that powder on top of crème will hinder blending, so always begin with the crème. It contradicts the rule of crème-on-crème, powder-on-powder---but it works.

Tip: You can also use your powder shadow as eyeliner. Simply apply it wet or dry using a brush.

Tip: Some powder shadows are harder pressed and more powdery, while others have a slight creamy texture.

all four types of shadows come in a variety of finishes.

MATTE is the best for creating a natural no-makeup look and is the most preferred finish for your midtone shade because of its natural appearance. It usually contains a higher level of color pigment and works really well for reshaping and defining the eye.

SHIMMER shadows offer great, sheer coverage so that when you sweep on the color, you can still see the skin underneath. Shimmer shadows have a subtle sheen and give a hint of sparkle. They typically won't collect in fine lines, which makes them a perfect choice for mature skin. Light shimmer shadows work great for highlighting and bringing out recessed areas of the eyelid. Dark shimmer shadows work great for adding drama without being as harsh as deep-tone matte shades.

FROST shadows give much more opaque coverage and feature a white or silver sparkle. They usually come in fun, light pastel shades that work best on younger skin. Frosted shadows can easily sink into wrinkles and therefore, do not work as well on mature skin.

SATIN falls perfectly in between matte and shimmer. It's shinier than matte, but not nearly as shiny as a shimmer. A satin finish works well on all skin types, including mature skin.

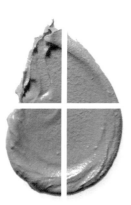

blush

usually comes in four different textures.

POWDER BLUSH is color pigment set in a powder base. Applied with a soft blush brush it gives a dusting of color that works well with all skin types. It's the most popular type of blush because it's the easiest to control and use – and it's usually available in the widest range of shades. Powder blush is the best choice for oily skin.

CRÈME BLUSH is color pigment set in a crème base. It has a fresh dewy finish that gives the face a luminous, natural glow. It is great on dry skin because it slides easily over the surface. It works best when applied before you powder because it will blend more easily. Unfortunately, if you have oily skin, crème blush is not your best choice because it won't wear well. And it doesn't work well on skin with large pores because it tends to accentuate them. It's great for those who don't need or want to wear foundation. Just apply it with your fingers or a sponge and work it into your skin.

GEL BLUSH is basically made up of color pigments that are wrapped within silicone particles. It will smooth very nicely onto bare skin to create a pretty, sheer, translucent glow. It's not to say you can't use it with foundation; you can. Just make sure you apply it before you powder. It's long lasting, looks very natural, and it's easy to use. You can use your fingers or a sponge to apply it, then smooth it into the skin.

LIQUID BLUSH is actually a liquid that stains the skin. It's terrific for all skin types. It's applied like the gel blush, but more difficult to work with because it must be blended quickly due to its staining quality. It's waterproof so you can expect it to last all day. Just like crème blush or gel blush, you can use either a sponge or your fingers to apply and blend it into your skin.

Tip: If you're using powder blush directly on bare skin, be sure to powder your face first to prevent it from looking splotchy.

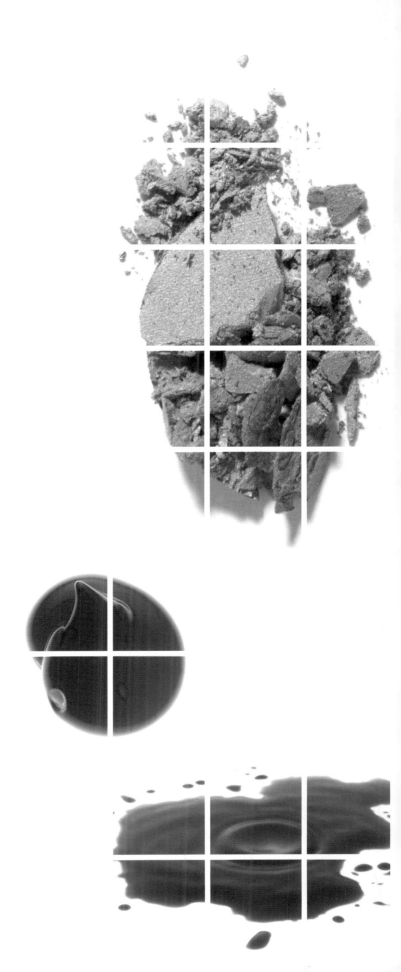

bronzer

is used to give the skin a warm, healthy glow. It usually comes in powder and crème formulas.

BRONZING POWDER. Like powder blush, it is the most popular because it's so easy to control and blend. It can come packaged in a variety of ways---pressed in a compact, loose in a tub, or even in a jar pressed into small balls or beads. Swept across strategic areas of the face with a brush, it can bring the skin to life.

CRÈME BRONZER. Like bronzing powder, it is used to give the face a sun-kissed glow. You can find it in the form of a stick or even in compacts. It can be applied with your fingers or a sponge. It's great on dry skin, or when you don't want to wear foundation but want that little extra glow.

lip stick

is available in a variety of formulas.

MATTE delivers sophisticated and intense full-coverage color that contains absolutely no shine. Because of its formulation it stays on longer, but it can be drying and may give your lips the feeling and appearance of being dehydrated. It is great in dark, intense shades because it stays put and won't smear, but it certainly does nothing to make the lips look younger or fuller.

CRÈME contains more emollients than matte lipstick and provides a full coverage of moist though not shiny color. Most cosmetic lines offer the largest selection in this formula because it is the most versatile and popular. It wears quite well without being as dehydrating as matte.

FROST provides a pale, shiny, metallic appearance. But because of the single color of sheen in the formula's ingredients, there is a tendency for the lips to appear a little dry. It usually gives very opaque coverage that's not wonderful for mature lips.

SHEER is actually a glossy, sheer color-wash that allows the natural lips to show through because it is not formulated to cover opaquely. It's similar to a gel blush because it is simply pigments mixed with a gel. It lasts longer than a gloss but not as long as a crème lipstick. It's terrific for a quick fix because due to its sheerness it doesn't have to be applied with exact precision.

GLOSS is a lip color with extreme shine and moisture. It delivers a sheer layer of color that is going to need frequent reapplication. Although it doesn't last too terribly long, gloss gives a fresh-and-alive look that's perfect for all age groups. Used correctly it can make the lips look fuller and sexier. You'll find it packaged in a wand, tube or pot.

LIPLINER is a pencil that's used to define your lips. It helps correct lip shapes as well as prevent lip color from bleeding into fine lines. It can also be used over the entire lip then topped with a color. Using a lipliner greatly improves the staying power of any lip color.

thetools

Just like a painter selects the right brush to create the perfect stroke, so does the makeup artist. And you can too, with a little help from me. In this chapter, I've featured the best, basic tools from my own brush collection to help you create the makeup effects you want. And remember makeup is like a work of art, an expression of your inner beauty. So experiment and have fun.

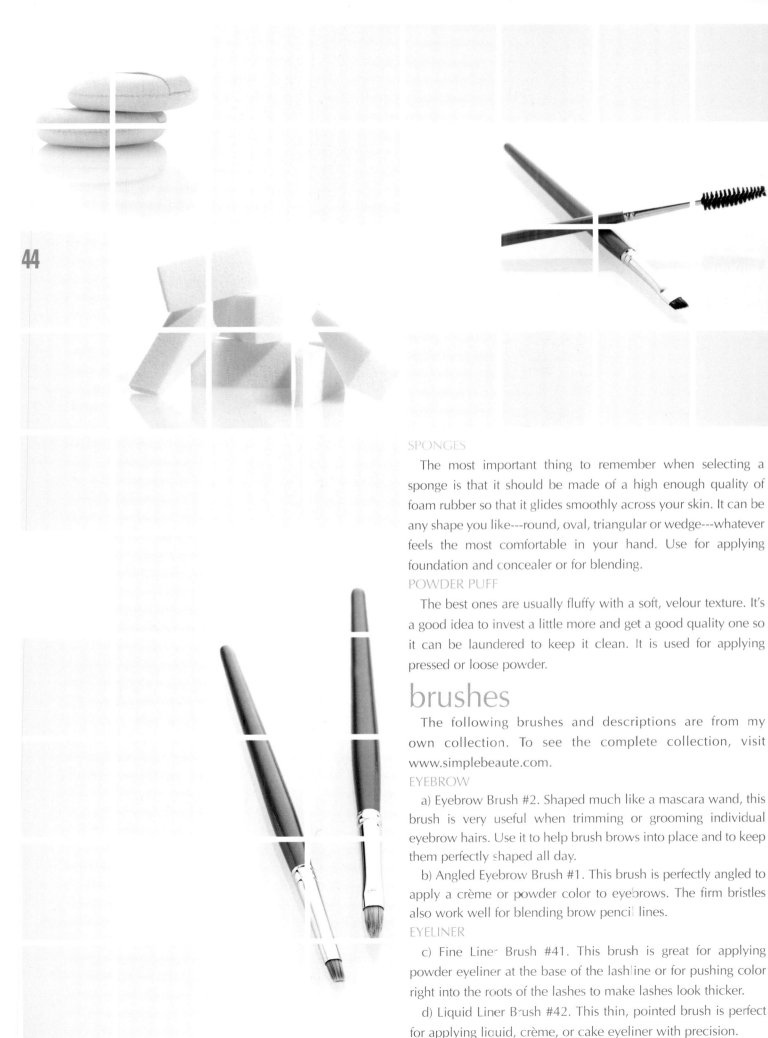

SPONGES

The most important thing to remember when selecting a sponge is that it should be made of a high enough quality of foam rubber so that it glides smoothly across your skin. It can be any shape you like---round, oval, triangular or wedge---whatever feels the most comfortable in your hand. Use for applying foundation and concealer or for blending.

POWDER PUFF

The best ones are usually fluffy with a soft, velour texture. It's a good idea to invest a little more and get a good quality one so it can be laundered to keep it clean. It is used for applying pressed or loose powder.

brushes

The following brushes and descriptions are from my own collection. To see the complete collection, visit www.simplebeaute.com.

EYEBROW

a) Eyebrow Brush #2. Shaped much like a mascara wand, this brush is very useful when trimming or grooming individual eyebrow hairs. Use it to help brush brows into place and to keep them perfectly shaped all day.

b) Angled Eyebrow Brush #1. This brush is perfectly angled to apply a crème or powder color to eyebrows. The firm bristles also work well for blending brow pencil lines.

EYELINER

c) Fine Liner Brush #41. This brush is great for applying powder eyeliner at the base of the lashline or for pushing color right into the roots of the lashes to make lashes look thicker.

d) Liquid Liner Brush #42. This thin, pointed brush is perfect for applying liquid, crème, or cake eyeliner with precision.

EYESHADOW

a) Eyeshadow Brush #13. This precision-style brush is perfect for applying your favorite shade of eye color along the lower lashline. Or use it to apply a very defined line of color into the crease of the eye.

b) Eyeshadow Brush #17. This firm, angled brush is great for applying your midtone color into the crease or for blending eyeshadow shades together.

c) Eyeshadow Brush #26. This large brush is great for applying midtone colors into the crease and for all-over blending of the eye colors – a must when you're wearing more than one eye color.

d) Eyeshadow Brush #12. This arched brush helps you precisely apply your most intense shade of eye color along your lashline and into the outer corners of the crease of your eyes.

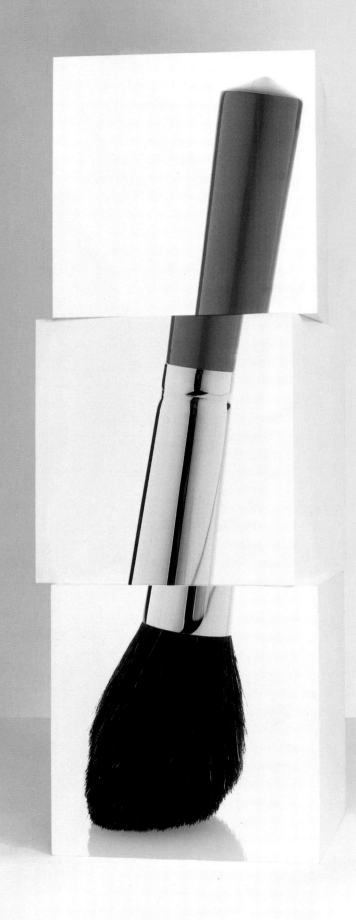

BLUSH (Opposite page)

Blush Brush #62. A full, soft brush that is great for applying blush or bronzer. Tapered toward the end to help you blend as you apply.

EYELASH CURLER

A tool used to curl the lashes which helps create the illusion of "opening up" the eyes. This is a must-have beauty tool for women of all ages.

BELOW:

a) Foundation Brush #51. A large, smooth brush to help you evenly apply crème or liquid foundation onto the skin. Perfect for end of the day touch-ups, it can help you create a smooth, even application over the foundation you may already be wearing.

b) Jumbo Powder Brush #70. This big and fluffy brush is great for applying loose powder for a smooth, sheer and even application.

c) Concealer Brush #50. This tapered brush is used for applying concealer with precision. It allows you to cover spots or flawed areas of the face without over-blending or over-working concealer.

d) Eyeliner Brush #40. The perfect brush to help you line and define your eyes with eyeshadow or for applying powder over your pencil eye liner to create a more natural, subtle look.

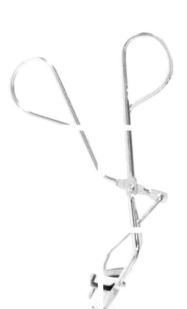

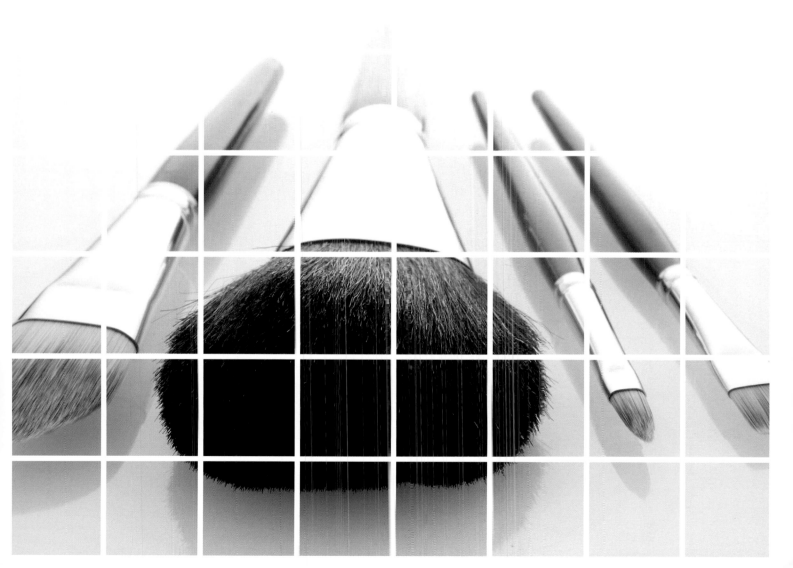

	shimmer	flesh	highlight
	shimmer	beige	highlight
	shimmer	gold	highlight
	matte	sand	highlight
	matte	taupe	midtone
	matte	rose	midtone
	matte	dark taupe	midtone
	matte	carmel	midtone
	matte	mahogany	midtone
	shimmer	golden brown	contour
	matte	dark brown	contour
	matte	burgundy	contour
	matte	black	contour

48

eyeshadows

To show you how simple but versatile makeup can be, I chose a basic eye shadow palette at left to create every before-and-after look in this book. I believe with this palette, any woman can look beautiful, regardless of her eye shape or whether she has ivory, beige, bronze or ebony skin tone. Notice that the shades fall into three categories: highlight, midtone and contour. Using these three depth categories of color helps give shape to your eyelids. To learn more about this simple application technique, turn to Page 134.

colorchoices

In this chapter my goal is to help you make educated choices in selecting your color products. Choosing the correct shade of foundation is so important since it can affect the overall look of your make-up, as can the wrong choice of eye shadow, blush and lipstick. Together, we can increase your chances of making the correct choices. Let's start the education process with a little foundation history.

All through the 1950s, until the late 1970s, women were told that it was correct to choose the opposite of their natural skin tone for their foundation color. For example, if your skin had olive undertones you used a pink-based foundation, and if your undertones were pink you used an orange-toned foundation.

And then in the 1980s, women were informed that this was all wrong and they should match their skin's exact undertone. So if you had pink undertones your foundation color had to be pink-based. If your undertones were olive, you put on an olive-toned foundation---well, you get the picture.

Then finally in the 1990s, the cosmetic industry discovered that yellow undertones, instead of being undesirable, actually made the skin look the most alive and natural. Yellow is the one color that everyone has in their skin, from the very lightest complexion to the darkest. It's just that some people have other colors in their skin as well, such as shades of red or brown. Almost everyone looks better with some yellow in their foundation. It counteracts the skin tones you don't want to see and enhances the tones that you do want to see.

skinchart

Let's try to make this simple.

There are approximately 15 levels of depth to the skin. "Depth" is the lightness or darkness of your skin, Level 1 being very pale (porcelain) and Level 15 being very dark (ebony). At each level there are basic undertones that are needed to make your skin look its best.

Eighty-five percent of all women are "warm." In my opinion, warmer skin always looks more youthful. Only about 15 percent of women are truly "cool." They have dark hair, pale skin and light eyes. (Think Snow White.) Even if you start out cool, the minute you go out into the sun, you become warm. If you come from an ethnic background -- Italian, Hispanic, Asian or African-American -- you're warm. If you have brown or green eyes, you're warm. If you are able to tan well, you're definitely warm.

One of the biggest makeup mistakes women make is thinking they have cool undertones when they don't. That's why it's always important to conduct a "stripe test" to make sure you're wearing the right foundation to match your skin depth level. On Page 59, you'll learn how to properly conduct a stripe test. Right now, use the chart and following model photos to help you identify the depth levels of your skin and the foundation shade that complements you best.

tone	depth level	
fair	1	
fair	2	
fair	3	
medium	4	
medium	5	
medium	6	
olive	7	
olive	8	
olive	9	
bronze	10	
bronze	11	
bronze	12	
ebony	13	
ebony	14	
ebony	15	

rhonda shasteen

SKIN LEVEL: 2 (fair)
FACE SHAPE: pear-shaped face
EYE SHAPE: close-set eyes
SHADOWS: Highlight-shimmer flesh
         Midtone-matte taupe
         Contour-shimmer golden brown

OBJECTIVE: to give the illusion of a more oval-shaped face. To visually pull the eyes apart.

APPLICATION: contoured the jawline and cheeks to minimize their width. Highlighted the forehead to create the illusion of more width. Highlighted the inner corner of eyelids to visually push the eyes apart. Defined the outer corners of eyes with the deepest shadow.

sherril steinman

SKIN LEVEL: 3 (fair)
FACE SHAPE: pear-shaped face
EYE SHAPE: hooded eyes
SHADOWS: Highlight-shimmer beige
         Midtone-matte taupe/matte dark taupe
         Contour-matte dark brown

OBJECTIVE: to give the illusion of a more oval-shaped face. To minimize the hooded appearance of the eyelids, making her eyes to appear more open.

APPLICATION: contoured the jawline and cheeks to minimize their width. Highlighted the forehead to create the illusion of more width. Using midtone and contour colors, applied, then blended them to the hooded area, giving the illusion that the area recedes.

linda bird

SKIN LEVEL: 5 (medium)
FACE SHAPE: pear-shaped face

SHADOWS: Highlight-shimmer beige
          Midtone-matte taupe
          Contour-shimmer golden brown
OBJECTIVE: to give the illusion of a more oval-shaped face.
APPLICATION: contoured the jawline and cheeks to minimize their width. Highlighted forehead to create the illusion of more width. Highlighted the eyelid to brighten the eye, then concentrated on defining the crease and the lashline.

michelle boye

SKIN LEVEL: 6 (medium)
FACE SHAPE: square-shaped face
EYE SHAPE: wide-set eyes
SHADOWS: Highlight-shimmer beige
          Midtone-matte dark taupe
          Contour-shimmer golden brown
OBJECTIVE: to give the illusion of a more oval-shaped face. To help it appear as if the eyes are closer together.
APPLICATION: contoured hairline and jawline to soften the "four corners". Highlighted down the center of the forehead, nose and chin. Applied a darker midtone to the inside hollow of her eyes, to visually pull the eye placement closer together.

eleanor simon

SKIN LEVEL: 7 (olive)
FACE SHAPE: oval-shaped face
EYE SHAPE: hooded eye
SHADOWS: Highlight-shimmer beige
        Midtone-matte taupe/matte dark taupe
        Contour-shimmer golden brown
OBJECTIVE: to minimize the hooded appearance of the eyelids, causing her eyes to appear more open and alive.
APPLICATION: applied midtone and contour color to the hooded area of the lids to help them recede and "open up" the eyes. Subtly layered color, starting with light and increasing to dark taupe, to the hooded area so as to create a more natural effect.

lydia duron

SKIN LEVEL: 3 (olive)
FACE SHAPE: square-shaped face
EYE SHAPE: hooded eyes
SHADOWS: Highlight-shimmer beige
        Midtone-matte dark taupe
        Contour-matte dark brown
OBJECTIVE: to give the illusion of a more oval-shaped face. To minimize the hooded appearance of her eyelids, causing her eyes to appear more open and alive.
APPLICATION: contoured the hairline and jaw to soften the "four corners". Highlighted down the center of the forehead, nose and the tip of the chin. Subtly layered color to the hooded areas to help minimize them. (Really beautiful brows are important with hooded eyes because they will draw attention up and away.)

sonja hunter mason

SKIN LEVEL: 12 (bronze)
FACE SHAPE: round-shaped face
EYE SHAPE: wide-set eyes
SHADOWS: Highlight-shimmer gold
    Midtone-matte mahogany
    Contour-dark burgundy

OBJECTIVE: to give the illusion of a more oval-shaped face. To even out skin tone and brighten areas to add life to the face.

APPLICATION: Using multiple shades of foundation, evened out skin tone then highlighted areas with a golden-orange face powder to give life to the skin. Softly sculpted her cheeks, jaw and temples. Highlighted the lid and contoured the inside hollow of eyes to visually pull them closer.

alischia butler

SKIN LEVEL: 15 (ebony)
FACE SHAPE: square-shaped face

SHADOWS: Highlight-shimmer gold
    Midtone-matte mahogany
    Contour-dark burgundy

OBJECTIVE: to give the illusion of a more oval-shaped face. To even out skin tone and brighten areas to add life to the face.

APPLICATION: using multiple shades of foundation, evened out the slight skin discoloration. The main goal was to brighten her face. Which was achieved by using a golden-orange face powder to highlight areas. Contoured hairline and jaw to soften the "four corners".

foundation

The best way to choose a foundation color is to conduct a stripe test. Here are a few fast rules to follow so you won't "flunk." Always conduct your stripe test in natural light. Start with three different foundation shades to compare and contrast. (The area where you will test the shades will vary depending on your skin tone.) Finally, if the shade you choose best matches your neck, you will pass the stripe test with flying colors.

IVORY AND BEIGE

Ivory and beige skin tones should conduct the stripe test from jaw to neck to get a true match to the neck. Women with these skin types tend to have redness in their faces, but not in their necks, so it's important to get a true match. Start by applying three stripes of the different foundation shades from your jaw to your neck and wait a few minutes to see if the oils in your skin change the color pigments. Select the one that most closely matches your neck.

BRONZE AND EBONY

Women with bronze and ebony skin tones should stripe test from the cheek area to the jaw area because some women with these skin tones have "facial masking," or lighter skin on the interior of the face and darker skin on the outer edges of the face. Start by applying three stripes of the different foundation shades extending from your cheek to your jaw area, and wait a few minutes to see if the oils in your skin change the color pigments.

If you have any degree of facial masking, I suggest using my technique of applying two shades of foundation to perfect your skin tone: One shade to brighten your skin, and another to deepen it. Turn to Page 90 to find out why two shades are better than one when it comes to facial masking and how to apply them.

CHOOSE YELLOW OVER PINK

As I said before, a shade of yellow foundation complements almost any skin tone. The only time pink is a better choice is if you have pink undertones in your neck as well as your face, which is very rare. Most women with pink in their face do not have it in their neck. Pink foundation on top of a pink face can become red -- and no one wants a red face. Foundations and powders with pink hues actually age the skin and make it appear unnatural, yet many mature women choose pink to give their face more color. Remember that color should be provided by your blush and lipstick – not by your foundation and powder.

Yellow foundations can actually counteract skin conditions such as rosacea and broken capillaries. Women with these conditions or with ruddy skin tones often feel that yellow foundations look too yellow because they're used to seeing all the red in their face. Give it time! Your skin will start to absorb the foundation and work with it better, and your eye will get used to seeing the red neutralized. You'll soon notice a more even, natural skin tone.

In contrast, many women with yellow in their skin will try to counteract that by choosing a pink foundation. This is never a good choice. You should embrace and enhance the yellow tones in your skin to make it appear younger, more fresh and alive.

Women with ebony skin should match the undertones in their skin exactly because they are so distinct and noticeable. They can range all the way from golden-orange to true brown. Keep in mind that it is always a good idea to brighten (not lighten) ebony skin. God gave you plenty of pigment, so it's best to brighten your face and bring it to life. Intense golden-orange tones work well for brightening ebony skin.

powder

IVORY AND BEIGE

As with foundation and concealer, a face powder with yellow or neutral undertones is usually the best choice. I never recommend using a face powder with pink undertones because it can make the skin appear artificial and older. Your goal should be to find a neutral shade of powder to match your foundation exactly. Or, if you want to warm up your skin or correct imperfections, you should choose a powder with yellow undertones.

BRONZE AND EBONY

Bronze and ebony skin tones should use a powder with golden-orange undertones to brighten and freshen the skin to a beautiful glow. The darker the skin, the more likely you should use a powder with warm-brown undertones to give the skin a glowing, natural look. Dark bronze and ebony skin tones also should choose a loose powder with a hint of shimmer to it. This will help absorb any oils in the skin and keep it looking fresh and dewy. Loose powders with a matte finish can make bronze and ebony skin appear very flat and ashy.

One more important point about powder: transluscent powder is not invisible, even though the word indicates that it is. It is less opaque than other powders, but it is not colorless and can often appear unnatural, especially on dark beige and olive skin tones. It's always best to choose a powder that is an appropriate match for your skin tone, or one that brightens your skin.

concealer

IVORY AND BEIGE

You can get a lot of mileage out of concealers with yellow undertones. Yellow is the best color choice because it works to counteract most skin imperfections, including the purple of undereye circles, the brown of age spots, and any ruddiness or red in the complexion. The more severe the imperfection, such as a port wine stain or extremely dark circles, the more yellow you will need in your concealer.

BRONZE AND EBONY

On bronze and ebony skin, a golden-orange concealer for lighter to medium skin tones works wonderfully. For really deep tones of ebony, a warm brown concealer usually covers best.

eye color	liner	shadow
blue	warm brown/taupe	rich warm browns/ warm taupes/ soft peaches
green	red-brown/taupe/ purple	golden browns/ warm taupes/ deep purples/ soft peaches/ soft violets
brown	rich brown/ charcoal/taupe/ purple	golden brown/blue/ green/light mahogany/ charcoal/purple
grey	charcoal/deep brown	charcoal/cool brown/ purple

eyeshadow

The most important thing to remember about choosing eye shadow is...YOU! Look at the color of your eyes. Consider your skin tone. Then select a shade that will bring out the natural color of your eyes. Your goal is to make your eye color "pop" or stand out - not compete with or diminish your natural color in any way.

The chart on the opposite page can help you select shades that will enhance your eyes. Notice there is no blue shade suggested for blue eyes or green shadows for green eyes. The key is to select a color opposite from your own eye color. For example, the opposite of blue eyes is a warm shade of brown, tawny or golden shades.

Brown-eyed girls have it best. They can experiment with a variety of colors and still enhance their natural eye color. So play away in purple, green, gold or brown. Any color looks beautiful around brown eyes.

Skin tone is another thing to consider. Women with dark ebony skin should not choose an eyeshadow that is too white or light. Likewise, women with fair, pale skin might want to stay away from eyeshadows that are too dark. Subtle, natural colors look better than dramatic contrasting shades – especially during the daytime.

Finally, do not match your eye makeup to your clothing. Makeup is an accessory to you, just like your clothing. Makeup is not an accessory to your clothing. Matching your makeup colors to your clothes can sometimes wash you out and may not always flatter your best features. Choose what looks best on you. Apply your makeup as if you're wearing white, just like the models in this book. That way your real beauty can shine through and not take a back seat to your clothing or eye makeup.

EYELINER

No matter your eye color, choose neutral shades of eyeliner, such as taupe, black or brown, to shape and define your eyes. Colored eyeliners can help draw attention to your eyes by making the color "pop," but I recommend saving them for when you want to make a more dramatic makeup statement.

blush

Blush can brighten your face and make it positively glow. The trick is to find a blush color that's natural and neutral but still brightens and adds life to the skin. The best way to decide what shade to wear is to take a quick jog around the block and see what natural color your cheeks blush.

For ivory or light beige skin tones, a blush with soft pink undertones is usually your best choice. As you mature, you may want to switch to a blush with peach undertones instead of pink to help your skin appear brighter and fresher. The color peach is a mature woman's best friend. It can warm and enhance the skin while pink often appears ashy and artificial on the skin as it ages.

Olive skin tones should use blush with warm undertones that have a richness or intensity so the color shows up on the skin, such as tawny shades of cinnamon or sunny copper. Ebony and bronze skin tones should also choose a blush with warm undertones, such as apricot or paprika, to give their skin a nice warm glow that appears natural. For a more dramatic look, bronze and ebony skin tones can choose a blush with brick red or red brown undertones for more intense color on the skin. The very best choice for all skin tones is to choose a blush that looks soft and natural and appears to give you a glow from within.

lips

When it comes to choosing a lip color, size definitely matters. If you have full, beautiful lips, you can wear darker shades as long as it complements your skin tone. Lighter shades of lip color should be worn on thin lips to make them look fuller. The chart on the opposite page can help you find the perfect lip shades for you.

Skin tone is very important to consider before choosing a lip color. Ivory skin tones should not wear chocolate brown lips because it can age you and appear unnatural -- a woman with ivory skin would never have that much brown in her lips. Bronze skin tones should not wear pale, frosty lip shades because it can make lips appear ashy and artificial. Here's one more thing to remember. Dark lip colors age you faster than any other makeup product. And warmer lip colors always make you appear younger because they bring out the warm tones in your skin. So lighten up and have fun with your lip color. The beauty of wearing lipstick is that it adds life to your face and makes it appear more healthy and alive.

skintones	lipsticks
fair	glossy, transparent pinks/ soft peach/honey/beige
medium	warm pinks/soft mocha/carmel/ delicate red/warm apricots/tangy peach
olive	strong red/deep rose/berry/toffee/ mahogany/rich warm apricots/brown red
ebony	deep brownish red/deep berry/ deep fushia/golden beige

6

canvasprep

Getting a flawless finish begins with a few simple tricks up front. From perfectly arched brows to skin that's been easily prepped for makeup application, you'll find that it doesn't take a lot to get results that everyone will see.

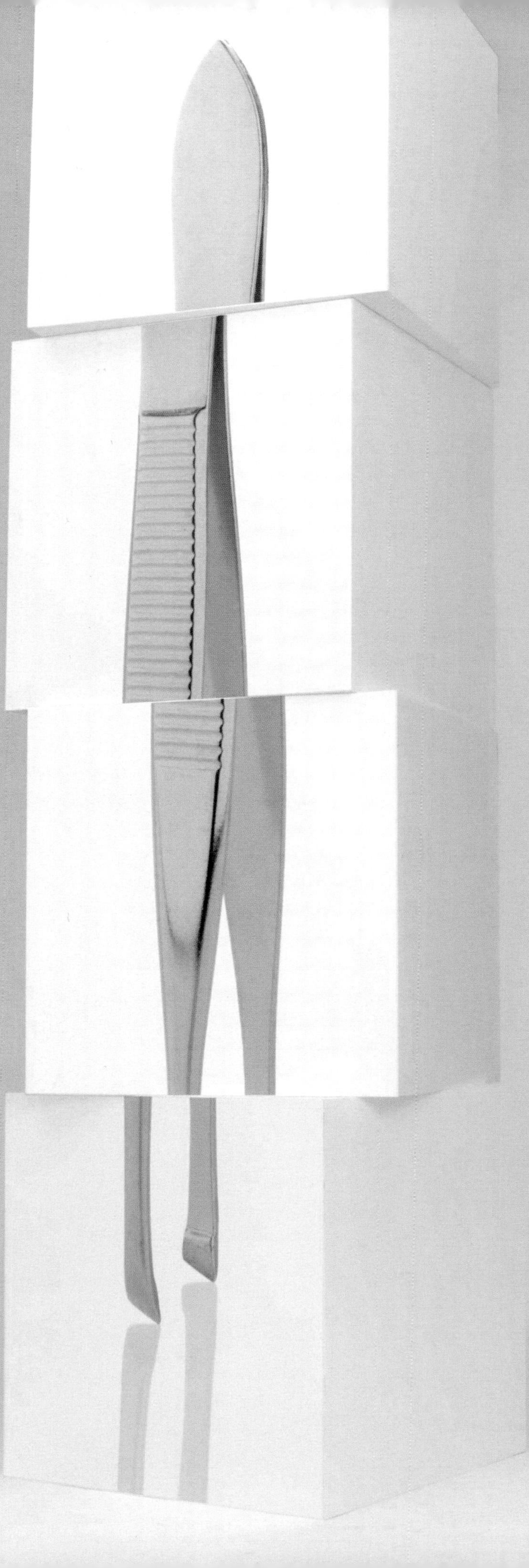

browattack

Well-groomed eyebrows are a beauty must. You should embrace your natural brow shape because no matter how much you tweeze, you cannot turn them into something they are not. Some brows naturally curve into a gentle arch; others grow straight across. The only way you can turn a straight brow into a curved one is by tweezing it away completely and drawing in a new one. But do not try this at home – or anywhere else! You'll find a simple, better way to find the best shape for your brows on the next few pages.

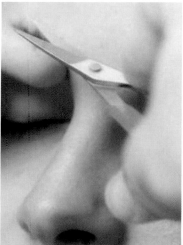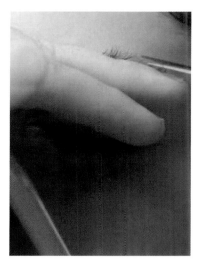

Before we begin, gather your tools together. You will need a pair of tweezers, a brow brush, a small pair of scissors and a white eye-pencil.

Now let's evaluate your brows.

First, are they too dense? Eyebrows that are too dense can be softened either by trimming them or lightening the color.

To trim them, simply brush them up and snip any stray hairs that extend past the upper brow line. Next, brush them down, and snip any unruly hairs that extend past the lower brow line.

Many times brow hairs are actually longer than they appear because the tips of the hairs are light in color and when they reach a certain length they tend to curl. By trimming them, you trim away some of the density and that slight curl so that the hairs lay down more neatly.

It's important to remember that if you need to trim your brows it should be done before you start to tweeze. Otherwise you might ruin your brow-line by tweezing away hairs that should have stayed but were simply too long.

Are your brows too pale, or are they speckled with grey? If they are, you might choose to have them tinted. It will help define them and alleviate the need for as much eyebrow makeup.

Now it's tweeze-time.

The best time to tweeze your brows is after a steamy shower when your skin is soft. It's a lot less painful because your pores are already open. Try to tweeze in natural light --you can see what you're doing so much better.

After plucking a couple of hairs from one brow, move to the other, then back and forth a few hairs at a time to guard the symmetry. Always tweeze in the same direction as the hair grows or the hair might not grow back lying properly.

HOW DO YOU DETERMINE WHERE TO START?

Here's how to make the perfect eyebrow take shape. Locate three pivotal points along your brow line by following this quick exercise:

Point A. Hold a pencil vertically against the side of your nose, noticing where it meets the brow. That is where your brow should begin.

Point B. Hold the pencil against your nostril and move it diagonally across the outer half of the iris of your eye. Notice where the pencil meets the brow. This is the best place for the peak of your arch. If you tweeze from Point A to Point B, tapering the line slightly thinner toward the peak, you will create the ideal shape for your brow.

Point C. Again, place the pencil against your nostril and extend it diagonally to the outer corner of your eye. Where it meets the brow is the best place for your brow to end. If you tweeze from Point B to Point C, tapering the line even thinner, you will create the best brow shape for your face.

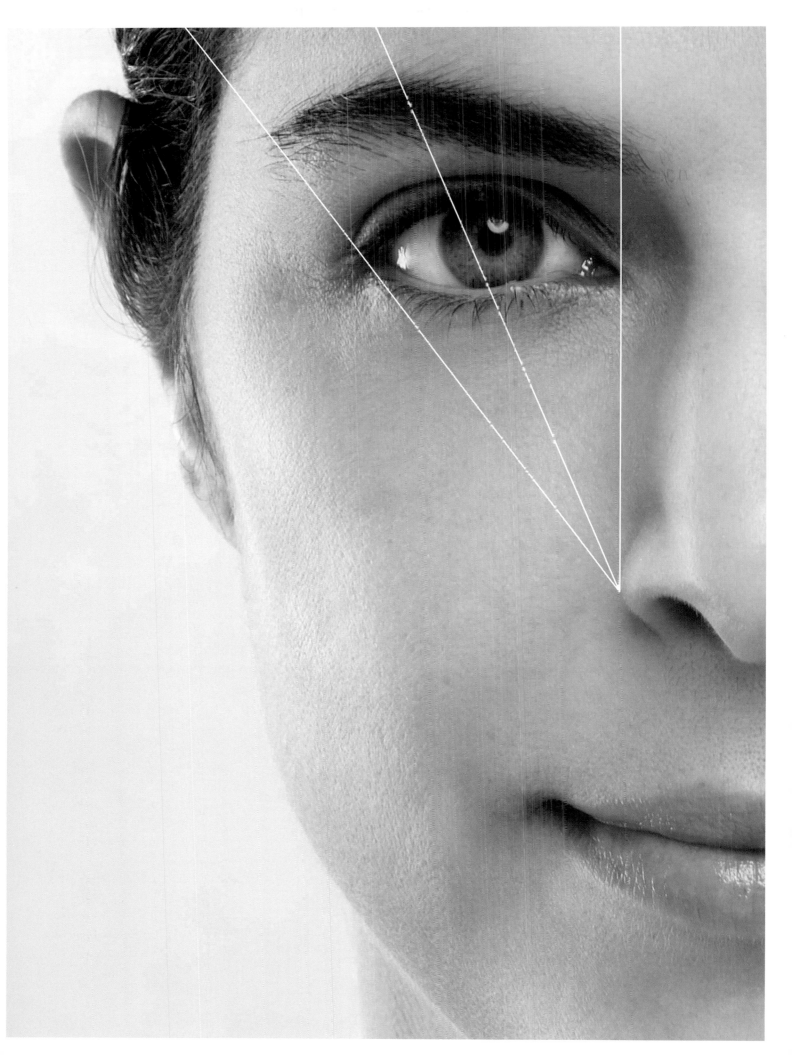

A great trick when preparing to tweeze is to use a white eye pencil to sketch a pattern-outline (a template of sorts) of the shape you want your brow to be. This is a great way to get a preview of the end result before you actually do the tweezing. It's then a simple matter of removing only the hairs that are covered in white.

> Tip: Take care not to overdo it because sparse brows, especially on a mature face, will make for a harder and older look.

> Tip: You can wax unwanted hairs, but be aware that the hairs may not grow back lying down correctly because wax is pulled off in the opposite direction of the hairs' growth. Also, a quick note: waxing repeatedly may eventually cause a crepe-like appearance to the skin.

moisturizer

Moisturizing is an important step that helps your foundation go on smoothly and evenly.

Make sure to begin with a freshly washed face, then apply your moisturizer. It's best applied to a damp face because it goes on more evenly. Moisturizer evens the skin's porosity and is most effective when it's left to absorb for a few minutes before you apply your makeup. You can use a light moisturizer or a heavy one; just make sure you choose the right one for your particular skin type.

Moisturizers for normal skin are usually light to help even out any dry areas.

Moisturizers for dry skin are usually higher in emollients and are richer.

Moisturizers for sensitive skin are fragrance-and irritant-free.

Moisturizers for oily skin are extremely light and won't clog pores. Many have oil-absorbing properties in them that actually help control the oil. Oily skin needs moisturizer because often, it can be over-dried by cleansers. The body is so smart, it actually produces more oil to compensate for the over-dryness, which only makes the complexion appear greasier. A light moisturizer keeps oily skin from producing more oil and can help even out its porosity.

primer

Primer is an optional makeup step that can do wonders for your skin's appearance. It helps your foundation go on more evenly and makes it last longer. Primer sometimes contains light-reflecting properties that reflect light and help diminish the appearance of some of your small flaws. So it can help your skin appear more perfect and stay fresh-looking all day. It also helps prevent your foundation color from altering due to your skin's natural oils because it creates a barrier between those natural oils and your foundation. Simply apply it on top of your moisturizer before you apply your foundation.

exfoliate

You should exfoliate your lips regularly to keep your lip texture smooth and soft. A great time to do this is right after you shower. Just apply a generous amount of lip balm and wait a few minutes for it to absorb. Using a soft bristle toothbrush, brush your lips vigorously then reapply more lip balm. If you prefer you can use a towel to rub your lips instead of a brush. Whichever method you use, always moisturize when you're finished. Exfoliating your lips regularly helps your lipstick go on more smoothly and helps your lips appear younger and smoother.

skindeep

We've all heard or even said, "My skin has a mind of its own." And in a way that's true. Everyone has a certain skin type with its very own characteristics. Once you know yours, it makes it easier for you to know which foundations are right for your skin type. See how simple it is to find your perfect match?

skintype	characteristics	needs	best foundation (texture)
dry	usually mature skin/ lacks emollients/ less elastic/ rarely breakout/ feels tight after cleansing/ usually small pores	moisturizing foundations/ formula containing emollients and anti-oxicents	tinted (moisturizer)/ liquid (moisturizing)/ mousse
normal	few to no breakouts/ neither to oily nor to dry/ medium pores/ smooth and even texture/ healthy color	ph balanced products	cream to powder/ tinted (moisturizer)/ liquid (all types)/ cream/ dual finish/ stick/ mousse
oily	prone to blackheads/ large pores/ get shiny fast/ breakout often/ wrinkles less/ usually highly elastic	oil-free products/ noncomedogenic/ products enrich with oil absorbers	cream to powder/ liquid (oil-free) (water-based)/ dual finish/ mousse
sensitive	burns easily (very)/ blotchy and dry patches/ more susceptible to rosacea/ sensitive to many products/ flush easily/ thin, delicate	hypo allergenic/ fragrance free/ moisturizing formulas/ formulas without chemical sunscreens	liquid (water-based)/ mousse/ tinted (moisturizer)/ dual finish

applying foundation

FOUNDATION

Selecting a foundation that's perfect for you will probably be one of your biggest makeup challenges. That's why I'm hoping the information I've given you so far can help make your selection a little easier. You'll also want to ask yourself the following questions before you set out to pick your perfect foundation:

1. What is my skin type?
2. What color of undertones do I have in my skin?
3. How much coverage do I want?
4. What type of finish do I want?

The answers should help you make the correct decision. It's also important to decide what type of finish you want (see below) because some work better on certain skin types than others.

**MATTE is a great choice for normal/oily skin. It works best on skin with imperfections such as breakouts, scars and discoloration. It gives you the best coverage and is perfect for oily skin because it contains no oils. However, use a light hand because if you apply it too heavily, it can appear mask-like.

**DEWY works great on dry skin because it adds moisture. It is wonderful for most skin types except oily skin, where it can increase the shine and showcase any flaws such as surface bumps or blemishes. Dewy foundation is not the best choice during summer or in high-humidity areas because it can appear too shiny or greasy instead of just dewy.

**SATIN works on almost all skin types, with the exception of excessively oily skin. It gives the skin a soft, smooth appearance. The finish is not as flat as matte, or as shiny as dewy, but falls in between the two. Satin is the most common foundation finish.

**LUMINOUS works well on any skin type. Its light-reflecting properties help hide tiny flaws and lines by reflecting light off the surface of the face.

When applying foundation you have three basic tools at your disposal.

• A sponge, which is the most sanitary because you can wash it or throw it away. Sponges also really help with the blending process.

• A brush blends well so it's great for touching up the foundation you've worn all day. It's always best to wash a sponge or a brush after every application. The cleaner the tool, the better the application.

• Don't have a brush or sponge handy? No problem because the third tool is your fingertips. Just make sure to wash your hands after you've applied your moisturizer and treatment products and before you apply your foundation. The residue from the treatment products can compromise the integrity of your foundation and diminish the amount of coverage it provides.

BASIC

It's best to begin your application on the center of your face, dotting foundation on the cheeks and the forehead then blending outward. Always remember to finish by blending downward to make sure all the small facial hairs lay flat. After application, blot with a tissue to absorb any oils left from the product. This will really help the staying power of your foundation. And don't forget to apply a light coat to the eyelids because it will help your eyeshadow glide on more easily and stay on longer. Be sure to finish with a light dusting of powder.

> Tip: The best way to achieve a natural look is to first go all over the face with a sheer foundation, then go back and dot your concealer on any small imperfections.

> Tip: Foundation can also be applied to your lips. It creates a blank canvas for any reshaping you want or need to do. It's also useful as an anchor for lipstick since it helps it stay on longer.

elaine moock

SKIN LEVEL: 3 (fair)
FACE SHAPE: square-shaped face
EYE SHAPE: hooded eyes
SHADOWS: Highlight-shimmer flesh
Midtone-matte taupe
Contour-matte dark taupe
OBJECTIVE: to give the illusion of a more oval-shaped face. To minimize the hooded appearance of her eyelids making the eyes to appear more open and alive.
APPLICATION: contoured hairline and jaw to soften the "four corners". Highlighted down the center of the forehead, nose, and the tip of the chin. Layered midtone and contour colors on hooded areas. The layering of color will help the end result look more subtle and natural.

pat smith

SKIN LEVEL: 10 (bronze)
FACE SHAPE: square-shaped face

SHADOWS: Highlight-shimmer gold
Midtone-matte mahogany
Contour-matte dark brown
OBJECTIVE: to give the illusion of a more oval-shaped face.
APPLICATION: contoured the hairline and jaw to soften the "four corners". Highlighted down the center of the forehead, nose, and tip of the chin. Highlighted the lid and brow bone. To create the definition at the lashline and in the crease, chose to layer the midtone color rather than a darker color.

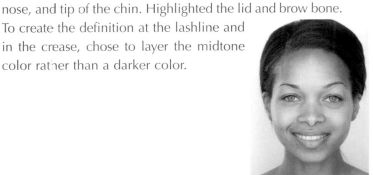

kerrie bodrato

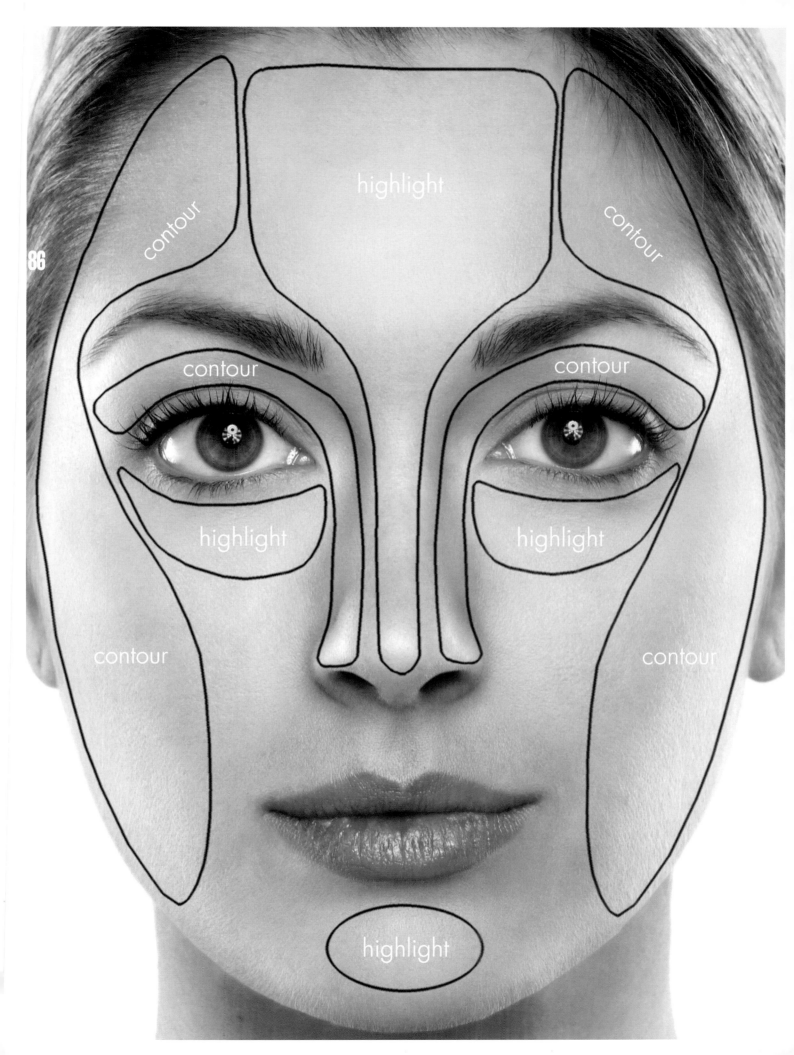

SCULPTING THE FACE

Many women with a full face want to make it appear slimmer. The most effective way to do this is to "sculpt" the face with foundation and powder. These tools can help make any face appear more oval – the face shape that is considered to be the most perfect.

No matter which products you choose, you will follow the same basic "sculpting" method. You will need to select three shades of foundation or powder in three different depth levels.

1. The first color should match your skin exactly. It is your true foundation color.

2. The second color, your highlight color, should be one level lighter than the first with the same undertone.

3. The third shade, your contour color, should be one level darker than your first with the same undertone. There should not be a dramatic difference between the three shades.

The diagram on the left will help you understand the purpose and placement of the three shades. You can also refer back to the face-shape diagrams in Chapter 8 starting on Page 102. Be sure to blend the three shades really well because it is the blending process that makes the sculpting method work.

1. Apply your first or true foundation color all over your face. Then visualize or trace an oval around your face. The width of the oval is your eye sockets; the height and length of your oval extends from the tip of your forehead to the tip of your chin.

2. Apply your second or highlight foundation color to the high points inside the oval, including your forehead, under the eyes on top of the cheekbones and the tip of your chin. This way, the features that you highlight will be what the human eye will focus on first.

3. Finally, use your contour or darkest shade and apply it to the areas outside the oval, including the temples, along your hairline and the sides of your cheeks. By deepening the outside areas, you are visually helping those areas recede, making your face appear more narrow and oval. If you have ivory or beige skin, you will contour your face more than highlight. On bronze and ebony skin, you will highlight your skin more than contour.

Here's an easy trick if you want to narrow the width of your nose. Just place the contour shade on the sides of your nose to make it appear narrower. If your nose is a little crooked, bring a straight line down on the top of your nose with the highlighter shade. People will naturally focus on the line, making the nose appear straight.

To complete your sculpted look, you can finish with three shades of powder: one that matches your true foundation shade, one that matches your highlighter shade, and a darker or bronzing powder to match your contour shade. This will give you a beautifully sculpted, three-dimensional effect that should make any face shape appear more oval.

Tip: Always remember to finish with a light dusting of powder to set your foundation.

88

tiffany mullen

patty woodrich

SKIN LEVEL: 2 (fair)
FACE SHAPE: pear-shaped face
EYE SHAPE: hooded eyes
SHADOWS: Highlight-shimmer flesh
Midtone-matte taupe
Contour-shimmer golden brown

OBJECTIVE: to create the illusion of a more oval-shaped face and to help her hooded eyelids recede.

APPLICATION: contoured jawline and cheeks to help minimize their width. Highlighted the center of the forehead to create the illusion of more width. Layered midtone and contour colors on hooded areas. The layering of color helps the end result appear more subtle and natural.

tracey allred

SKIN LEVEL: 4 (medium)
FACE SHAPE: pear-shaped face

SHADOWS: Highlight- shimmer flesh
Midtone-matte rose
Contour-shimmer golden brown

OBJECTIVE: to create the illusion of a more oval-shaped face and to help her hooded eyelids recede.

APPLICATION: contoured jawline and cheeks to help minimize their width. Highlighted the center of the forehead to create the illusion of more width. Highlighted eyelids and brow bones to open the eyes. Defined the crease and lashline.

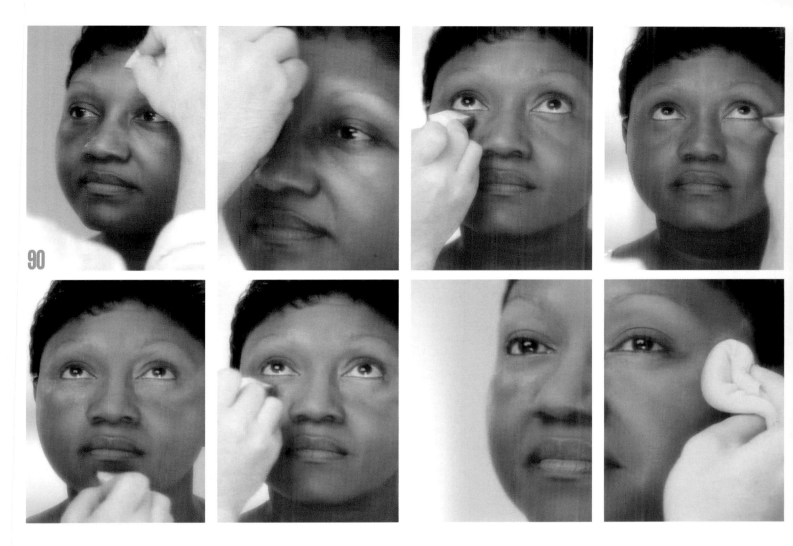

facialmasking

If your skin has a natural "mask" to it, that is, it has a tendency to be darker around the outer edges of the face and lighter on the interior of the face, you have a condition called facial masking, which sometimes occurs in women with bronze and ebony skin tones. With a little practice, it's easy to correct facial masking by using the following simple application techniques:

1. As I stated on Page 59, it's essential to conduct a stripe test across the cheek and the jaw to determine the two foundation shades you will need to create a more even look. It takes two foundation shades to correct your facial masking: one to brighten the darker areas and one to deepen the lighter areas. The goal of your stripe test is to find the two shades that, when applied to the opposite areas of your skin, meet in between and give you a more even skin tone.

2. Apply the lightest shade to the darker areas and blend well.

3. Apply the darkest shade to the lighter areas and blend well.

4. Finish with the face sculpting technique described on Page 87, using two loose powders – one to match your natural color and one to highlight the "oval" on your face, including your forehead, under the eyes on top of the cheekbones, and the tip of your chin.

phyllis r. sammons

maxine allen

SKIN LEVEL: 12 (bronze)
FACE SHAPE: oval-shaped face
EYE SHAPE: droopy eyes
SHADOWS: Highlight-matte sand
Midtone-matte carmel
Contour-matte dark brown

OBJECTIVE: to even out skin tone and brighten areas to help add life to the skin. To make the outer corners of the eye appear to turn up rather than down.

APPLICATION: evened out skin tone by using multiple shades of foundation. Brightened the skin with a golden-orange face powder on all highlighted areas of the face. Applied the midtone and contour shadows slightly in from the outside cornersof the eyes to draw attention to the center of the eyelids. Blended shadows well.

kim henry

SKIN LEVEL: 13 (ebony)
FACE SHAPE: square-shaped face

SHADOWS: Highlight-matte sand
Midtone-matte mahogany
Contour-dark burgundy

OBJECTIVE: to even out skin tone and brighten areas to help add life to the skin. To give face a more oval illusion.

APPLICATION: evened out skin tone by using multiple shades of foundation. Brightened the skin with a golden-orange face powder on all highlighted areas of the face. Contoured the hairline and jaw to soften the "four corners." Highlighted the center of the forehead, nose, and tip of the chin. Highlighted the lid and browbone to open up the eye. Defined the crease and lashline to give the eye more shape.

93

gloria mayfield-banks

concealer

Concealer can improve your skin's appearance dramatically, but only if it's invisible. The secret to covering under-eye discoloration (which is really blood vessels that appear blue or grey when they reflect light) is choosing the perfect shade and texture. If you use a formula that is too moist it can "travel", slipping into creases and fine lines, drawing attention to what you don't want people to notice. A formula that is too dry is bad for the delicate skin around the eyes and can draw attention to those same flaws. You might need to experiment to find the perfect formula for you. You should choose the same shade as your foundation, or a shade or two lighter if you have truly dark under-eye circles.

If you're using a concealer that matches your foundation exactly you may apply it either before or after your foundation. But if you're using one that is lighter, it is best to apply it first.

darkcircles

First prepare the area underneath the eye by applying eye crème and letting it soak in for two or three minutes. Blot away any excess with a sponge or tissue. Using eye crème will help your concealer adhere and if the skin under your eyes tends to be dry, your concealer won't "cake up" and give you an undesirable appearance. Remember, the undereye area contains less oil glands than anywhere else on your body, so it needs plenty of moisture. Be generous with your eye crème because it's next to impossible to "over-moisturize" the area. Just be sure to blot off any excess crème after a few minutes to make sure your concealer stays put.

Next, take a brush and apply concealer along the line of demarcation – where the discoloration begins on your skin. Extend the concealer up and over the discolored area with the brush. You never want to apply the concealer below the line of demarcation. If you do, you will lighten skin that is already the correct color and you'll be back where you started – with two uneven shades of skin. Next, take your finger and using a stippling motion, pat the concealer along the line of demarcation to blend it in. Be sure to conceal any darkness in the corners of your eyes or eyelids if necessary.

Serious dark circles call for serious concealer. Use a shade or two lighter than your foundation and apply the concealer before your foundation. When applying your foundation, be sure to stipple or pat it on over the concealed area. You don't want to wipe away what you initially applied. Yellow concealers are a great choice for covering dark circles on ivory and beige skin. And golden-orange concealers work great for covering dark circles on bronze and ebony skin. Both concealers can counteract all shades of skin discolorations, from red to purple to brown.

Tip: If you have mature skin, concealer and heavy powder can settle into under-eye lines and wrinkles. Since you won't want to accentuate them with too much powder, use your fingertip to dab on just the tiniest trace.

rebecca roome

under-eye puffiness

As painful as it is to admit this, you cannot improve the appearance of undereye puffiness by swiping a light concealer under the eye area. By now we know that anything we highlight on the face makes it stand out more. Our goal is to disguise the puffy area – not make it more prominent.

You can outsmart the puffy area by highlighting the area just underneath it. Because our faces are lit from above, the puffy area creates a shadow on the face. By highlighting the shadowy area, you will bring it out and make the puffiness recede. Because most people look directly at you and not from above, your puffiness will appear even with the rest of your skin. Voilà - you're flawless!

To apply, take a fine-tipped brush and apply the concealer just underneath the puffy area. Then lightly blend it with your finger, using a stippling motion. If you have dark circles as well as puffiness, which many women do, you'll want to use this three-step application:

1. Apply concealer to your dark circles first.
2. Next, apply your foundation to the rest of your face.
3. Then highlight underneath the puffiness with your concealer. This is one time that you will apply a lighter concealer after your foundation and not completely blend it away. Be sure and use a stippling motion to blend well.

> Tip: Using a concealer that's too light will only draw attention to what you're trying to cover.

> Tip: Concealer can be made sheerer by mixing it with a little eye-crème.

> Tip: You can test coverage by applying a little concealer to a vein on the inside of your wrist.

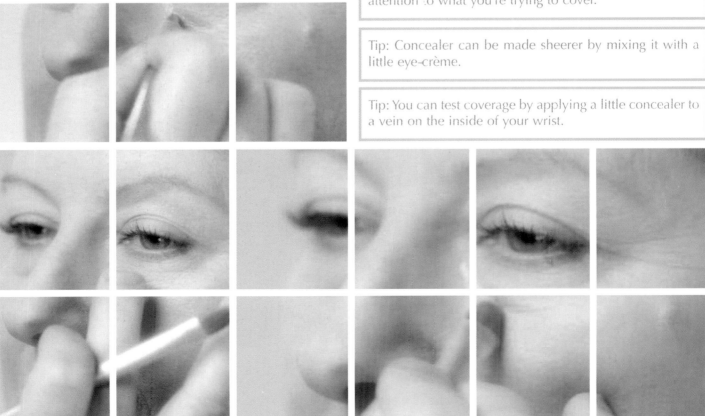

madeleine zeisler

skin imperfections

Let's face it: very few women have perfectly flawless skin. Yet many women are obsessed with perfection! Everything from sun damage to genetics can affect the surface of your complexion. Fortunately, there are several different concealers with different textures to help you tackle your problem areas and help your skin look its best.

blemishes

To minimize facial blemishes, you'll want to use a dry textured concealer so it will cling better to the blemish and not irritate or initiate more breakouts. Apply your foundation first and make sure to choose a concealer that matches your skin exactly. (A light concealer will only make the blemish seem larger.) Using a brush, apply the concealer directly to the blemish. Then take your finger and using a stippling motion, blend the edges around the blemish into the skin.

broken capillaries/ veins

Here, as always, it's important to apply concealer only to the areas of discoloration. You can take a brush and actually draw a line of concealer on top of the broken capillary or vein. Then stipple out the edges to blend. Pencil concealer also works great because it makes it so easy to draw the line.

rosacea

To counteract the redness of rosacea, you should use a yellow-based concealer and apply it only to the reddened areas of your face. Then stipple the outer edges with your fingertips and gently blend into skin. Do not overblend or you will move all of the concealer off of what you're trying to cover.

Tip: Yellow-based shades look healthier and more natural.

Tip: Using corrective green, pink or violet concealers will only turn your face colors.

Tip: To get that perfect shade of concealer, try mixing it with a little of your foundation.

hyper-pigmentation/ melasma

Age spots or brown spots can be caused by too much sun or by a shift in hormones during pregnancy. Hyperpigmentation or melasma can happen to women with any skin tone. To correct it, you'll want to apply concealer only to the areas that are discolored. Otherwise, if you extend the concealer past the line of demarcation, you will lighten skin that is already the correct color. After applying, you'll want to stipple the edges to blend the concealer. Finish by stippling foundation over the area so it will match your skin tone exactly. Ivory and beige skin tones should use an intense yellow concealer. Bronze and ebony skin tones should use a golden-orange concealer.

scars

A scar is a raised area of skin that has no pores, which makes it difficult to conceal because pores are what makeup clings to on the skin. To conceal a scar, apply a drier-textured concealer with a brush directly onto the scar. Then stipple the edges to blend it in. If you don't have a dry concealer for scars, try this treatment. Apply moisturizer to the scarred area followed by a bit of loose powder. The moisturizer gives the powder something to cling to. Then take a brush and apply concealer right on to the scar. The concealer and the powder mix together to form a drier texture that will stick better to the scar.

Remember that concealers are very different from foundations. They are drier, more heavily pigmented, and they "grab" powder differently. It's best to use a lighter shade of powder just on your concealed areas. If you use the same shade of powder as on the rest of your face, the concealed area may appear darker.

ann brown

powder

Powder is a makeup must. It sets your foundation, polishes off your look and adds a smooth, velvety softness to the skin. Because loose powder contains more oil absorbers, I personally like to use it to set the foundation and use pressed powder for touch-ups throughout the day. There are several ways to apply both types of powder:

• A sponge works well for tight areas and is great for "spot" powdering.

• A brush is the easiest and most commonly used tool. It is great for blending but you must be careful not to overblend and brush off what you apply. For best results, apply a little bit of powder at a time with a brush instead of all at once to ensure smooth, even coverage.

• A powder puff offers the best coverage and is my favorite way to apply powder. Press a puff or sponge into the powder and then "roll" it onto the skin. Pushing it into the skin makes your foundation and powder appear as one with your skin and looks far more natural. To finish, lightly sweep the face with a brush using gentle, downward strokes to remove any excess powder.

• A fingertip application works well for a light powder application. It's a great way to powder underneath the eyes, especially for mature women. Just dip your finger in loose powder. Rub your finger in the palm of your hand to brush off the excess, then trace your finger over the area underneath the eyes to set your concealer and help minimize fine lines.

faceshape

8

Everything about your face is unique, including its shape. So why would you want to put on your makeup the same as everyone else? Here, I'll show you the different face shapes and teach you how to apply your makeup to enhance the real you.

jamie cruise-vrini

ovalface

An oval-shaped face is considered by most to be the perfect facial shape because of its beautiful symmetry. It is usually broader at the cheeks, tapering in slightly at both the forehead and the chin. Because of its symmetry, you do not need to contour and highlight the face. You can experiment and play all you want. An oval face can support most makeup trends – so have fun.

106

carol aaron

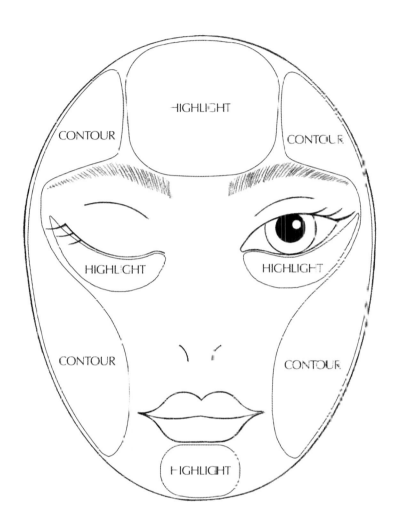

round face

A round-shaped face is fuller and generally holds its youthful appearance longer than the other face shapes. It's shorter, fairly wide, with full cheeks and a rounded chin.
If you have a round-shaped face:

*Highlight your forehead, underneath the eyes or top of the cheekbones and the center of your chin to draw attention to the center of your face.

*Contour your temples, cheeks and jawline with a bronzer or product that is one or two levels darker than your skin tone to create the illusion of an oval.

108

gayle kolsrud

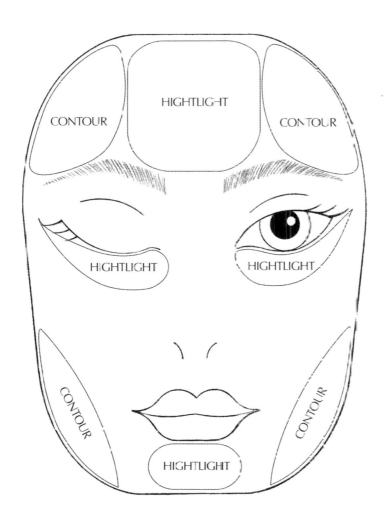

squareface

I personally consider this shape to be one of the most beautiful and the most photogenic because it suggests strength, and the features are usually symmetrically balanced. A square-shaped face is the same width at the forehead, the cheeks and the jaw.

If you have a square-shaped face:

*Highlight down the center of your forehead, underneath the eyes on top of the cheekbones and the tip of your chin to draw attention to the middle of your face.

*Contour your hairline at the two corners by your temples and the jaw at the two corners.

*Apply blush on the apples of your cheeks to help draw attention away from the corners of the square and help widen the area and make it appear more oval.

110

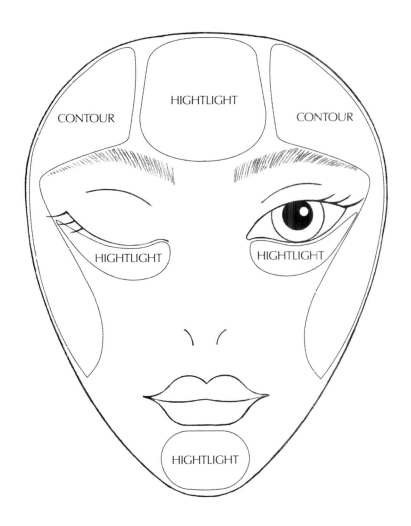

CONTOUR HIGHTLIGHT CONTOUR

HIGHTLIGHT HIGHTLIGHT

HIGHTLIGHT

heart-shapedface

The heart-shaped face is wide at the forehead and curves down to a pointed or narrow chin, similar to an inverted triangle. If you have a heart-shaped face:

*Highlight the chin to help broaden it. Highlight the forehead and underneath the eyes on top of the cheekbones to draw attention to the center of your face.

*Contour the temples and cheeks to diminish the width of this portion of your face.

Tip: Pressed powder works well for sculpting the face because it's low in pigment and blends easily – or if you like, you could use a bronzer; just be sure to blend really well.

kathy peel

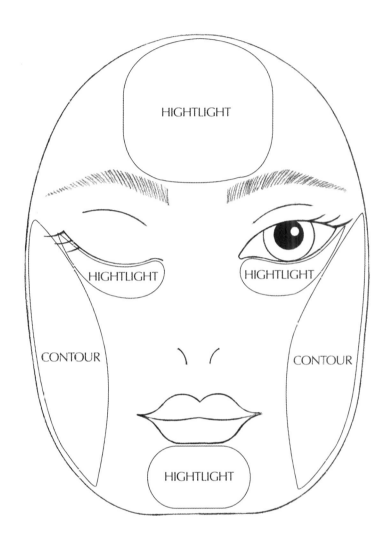

HIGHTLIGHT

HIGHTLIGHT

HIGHTLIGHT

CONTOUR

CONTOUR

HIGHTLIGHT

pear-shapedface

The pear-shaped face is narrow at the temples and forehead, and wider at the jawline.

If you have a pear-shaped face:

*Highlight your forehead to create the illusion of width, and highlight underneath the eyes on top of the cheekbones and the tip of your chin.

*Contour the jawline and the cheeks to minimize their width.

Tip: Remember that the proper hairstyle can go a long way in balancing any face shape.

karen piro

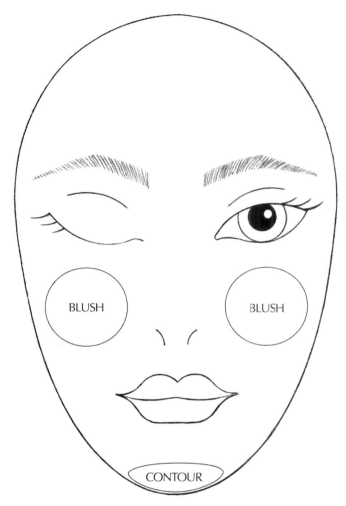

longface

The long-shaped face has high cheekbones, a high, deep forehead and a strong, sharp, chiseled jawline.

If you have a long face:

*Never highlight or contour your face. This will only make your face appear even longer.

*Brush a bit of bronzer across your chin to help shorten its length.

*Be generous with your blush and place a lot of color on the apples of your cheeks. This will help widen and shorten your face.

*Bangs can also help shorten the length of your face as well.

Tip: When applying your blush, start closer in on the apples of the cheeks and brush outward across the face.

michelle muslin

eyeshape

9

To master the art of eye color application, it's helpful to understand how the shape of your eyes can determine the placement of color and the effect it creates. Together, we'll look at a variety of different eye shapes and application techniques developed to maximize the individuality and beauty of each. Prepare to see the world of eye color application in a whole new way.

118

susan freeman

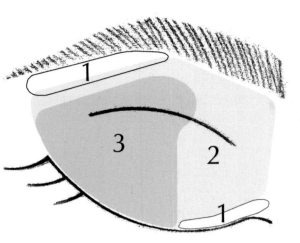

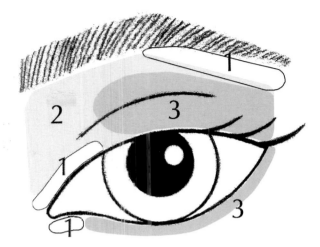

hoodedeyes

Hooded eyes are sometimes called "bedroom eyes" because the lids tend to look partly closed. Applied correctly, eye color can help hooded eyes appear more open by minimizing the eyelid. Our goal is to make the fleshy lid area "push away" or recede, and help your eyes become more prominent than the eyelids.

*Never use a dark eyeshadow over the entire lid because it makes it appear heavier and will close in your eyes.

*Don't be tempted to highlight the browbone too much because doing so can accentuate the hooded appearance of the eyelid.

Application (see diagram):

1. Highlight shade: Apply to browbone and along the upper lashline.

2. Midtone shade: Start at the base of your upper lashline and bring the color up and over the entire hooded area. This helps the lid recede. Make sure to blend the areas where the midtone color meets the highlight color.

3. Contour shade: Start at the base of the lashline and bring the color up and over the hooded area. This is one eye shape that you will bring your contour color in a little further and up a little higher than on other eye shapes. This will help the hooded area recede. Next, sweep the contour color underneath the lower lashes to define the lower lashline. You don't want to miss this step! Hooded eyes really benefit from a well-defined lashline, upper and lower.

Tip: The eyebrow shape is very important here because attention can be diverted from the hooded eyelid with a beautifully done eyebrow.

pam shaw

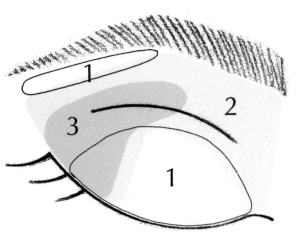

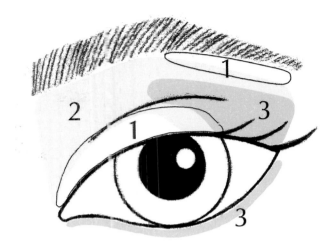

wide-seteyes

If the spacing between your eyes is wider than the width of one eye, your eyes are considered wide-set. Your goal is to create the illusion that they are set closer together.

*This is one instance where you will darken the inside hollows of your eye next to the bridge of your nose, more than any other eye shape. Deepening the color helps this area appear to recede and makes your eyes look closer together.

*Begin all dark color application slightly in from the outer corners and blend your shadow in and up instead of outward because this will "pull" the eyes wider apart, and your goal is to "pull" them closer together.

APPLICATION (see diagram):

1. Highlight shade: Apply to browbone and lid.

2. Midtone shade: Starting from the outer corner of the crease, bring the color towards the inside corner of your eye. Be sure to apply a few more layers to the inside corners to deepen the color and help visually push the eyes closer together.

3. Contour shade: Starting slightly in from the outer corner, brush it across the upper lashline and up into the crease of your eye. Also sweep it underneath the lower lashline, being careful not to extend the color beyond the outer edge of the eye.

122

missy brumley

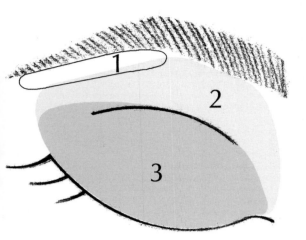

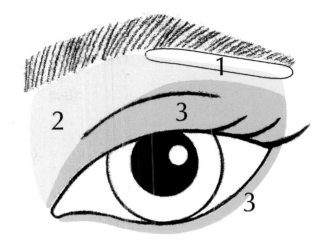

prominenteyes

If your eyelids and eyes are very full and tend to extend from the face, you have prominent eyes. The goal here is to visually "push" the eye away from us and help it appear to recede more gently into the face. We do this by creating a light-to-dark effect with the three eyeshadows, with the darkest shade applied closest to the lashline and fading as you go toward the brow.

*Never highlight the eyelid or you will make the eye appear even more prominent.

*A deeper or contour shade across the lid helps to minimize it and makes it appear to recede.

APPLICATION (see diagram):

1. Highlight shade: Apply to browbone only.
2. Midtone shade: Start at the base of your upper lashline and bring the color up and over your entire lid – all the way up to your browbone.
3. Contour shade: Again, start at the base of your lashline and bring the color all the way across the lid and up into the crease. Now sweep the contour color underneath the lower lashline as well.

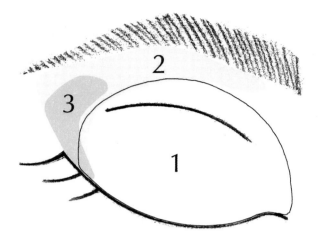

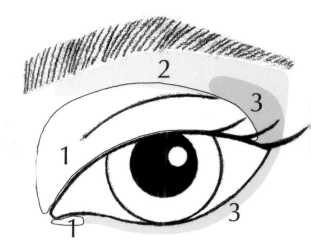

deep-set eyes

Deep-set eyes are eyes that are set deep into the sockets and the browbone extends out farther than any other eye shape. The goal with deep-set eyes is to bring them out and make them more noticeable.

*A dark eyelid does not work with this eye shape. You want to highlight deep-set eyes as much as possible to help bring them out.

*A dark crease is also unnecessary for this eye shape. Nature has provided its own, so there's no need to emphasize it.

*There is no need to highlight the browbone, since it is already prominent.

*If you wear eyeliner with this eye shape, keep it very close to the lashline and very thin. A thick eyeliner will work against you when you're trying to bring the eye out, especially on the upper lid.

APPLICATION (see diagram):
1. Highlight shade: Apply to the eyelid.
2. Midtone shade: Bring the color up above the crease and sweep it across the browbone to help visually "push" the browbone away from us.
3. Contour shade: Apply to the outer corner of the upper lashline, then up onto the corner of the browbone to help "push" the area away, or recede. Sweep the contour shade underneath the lower lashline for definition.

Tip: Never do a dark lid because it can close in your eye and make it appear smaller.

Tip: For drama, I always use a brighter (not necessarily a darker) color of shadow.

judie mᶜcoy

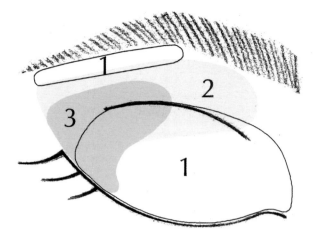

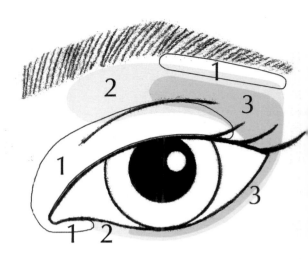

close-set eyes

The average space between a pair of eyes is approximately the width of one eye. If your eyes are spaced any closer, you have close-set eyes. Your goal is to create the illusion of them being farther apart.

*Keep the inside corners and areas closest to the nose as light as possible to help visually "push" the eyes apart.

*Make sure to concentrate the darker shades on the outer corners of this eye shape.

APPLICATION (see diagram):

1. Highlight shade: Apply to lid and browbone.

2. Midtone shade: Starting at the outer corner of the crease, bring the color in toward the inside corner to the brow but not all the way over to your nose.

3. Contour shade: Sweep it across the base of the upper lashline and up into the outer area of the crease. Sweep it underneath the lower lashline for definition, except for the inside corners. Apply your highlight shade to the inside corners of the eye to help your eyes appear farther apart.

Tip: To open up your eyes and create the illusion of them appearing larger, you can apply white or beige eyeliner around the inside "wet tissue" of the eyes.

taylor moore

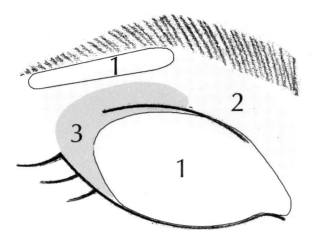

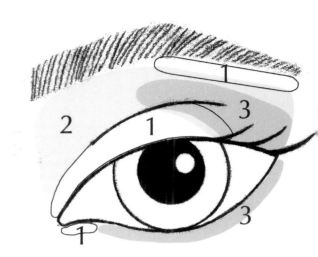

droopyeyes

Droopy eyes slope downward at the outer corners. They are sometimes referred to as "sad puppy dog eyes." Your goal is to make the outer corners appear as if they turn up rather than down.
*You can do this best by creating an "open-ended" eye, which means you do not extend your colors to the outer corner of the eye where it begins to turn down. By leaving it natural, you actually create a visual "lift" to the eye.
* When applying mascara, be sure to concentrate on the middle to inside lashes. Defined lashes on the outer corner of the eye will only accentuate the droopiness.
*Make sure your eyebrows curve outward, gently – never in an exaggerated downward arch.
APPLICATION (see diagram):
1. Highlight shade: Apply to browbone and lid.
2. Midtone shade: Starting slightly in from the outside corner, bring the color across the crease into the inside corner of the crease.
3. Contour shade: Starting in just slightly from the outside corner, bring your color up and into the crease. Next sweep contour color along the lower lashline making sure once again to start in slightly from the outside corner.

Tip: If you want to wear color at the lower lashline, begin your application about an eighth-of-an-inch in from the outermost corner.

129

lisa madson

basic application

10

Girls just want to have fun – especially when it comes to makeup. So get ready to play with color. On the next several pages we'll paint on the perfect eye look, learn the tricks of applying blush and bronzers, make lips speak volumes with luscious color and even experiment with false eyelashes. Get ready to reveal the real you.

132

sunni smyth

brows

When selecting a brow color choose one that is either your natural color or one shade lighter. Be careful not to confuse brow-pencils and powders with eye-pencils and shadows---they are not the same.

Brow-pencils are duller in color, usually with no sheen, and have a little more wax in their texture than do eyeliner pencils. Eyebrow powder is duller and more matte than eye shadow.

When using a brow-pencil, apply short, feathery, hair-like strokes angled in the same direction as the hairs' growth. Never draw on a solid, hard-looking line. Short feather-like strokes are meant to imitate short little hairs. I prefer to go over the area again, using a small angled brush, following the same stroke pattern. It blends it in a little better and helps it appear more natural.

You can also achieve a very natural brow by using brow-powder. Apply it with a small, stiff, angled brush in short, feathery strokes while following the natural hair-growth pattern.

For those with scars or brows that are just not there, you may need the coverage of a crème brow-color. It gives the most coverage. Simply apply it with a stiff, angled brush using short feathery strokes. It's always best to follow crème with a brow-powder to set it and help it last all day.

Whichever method you prefer, when grooming your brows, always finish by using a brow brush to brush upward and outward. If you like, you can end with a brow gel. It acts like hairspray for the brows. To review how to find the best shape for your brows, turn to Page 72.

Tip: Sharpen your pencil each time you use it.

Tip: You can use eyebrow pencil or eyebrow powder separately, or you can combine them. If you combine them, you'll increase their wearing time.

eyes

Three is definitely a charm when it comes to applying eye color. It takes three shades to shape the eye: a highlight, midtone and contour shade. The basic rule to remember is that everything you highlight will come toward you or become more prominent. And everything you contour or darken will recede or move away from you. Using three shades creates a subtle visual trick to help bring out one of your most beautiful features and help draw attention to your eyes rather than the eyelids. While there are thousands of shades to choose from, everyone should use the three-shade application technique for best results. Be sure to review Pages 116-129 to identify your particular eye shape and learn the correct placement for your three shades.

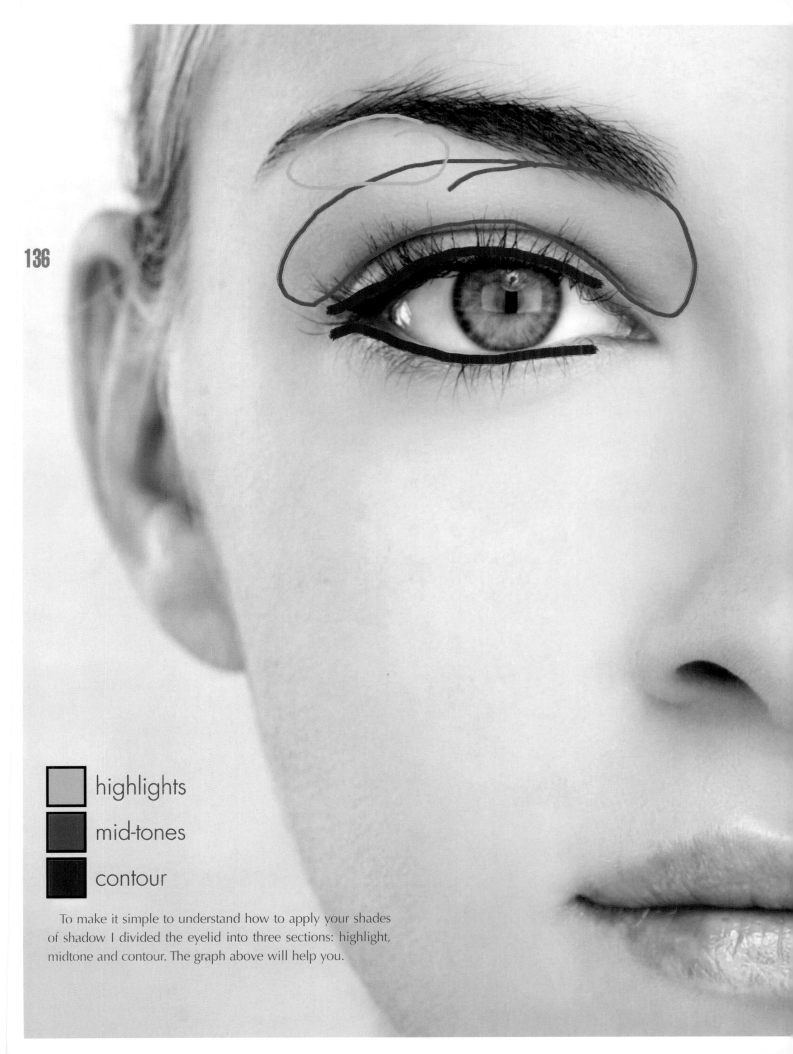

136

136

highlights

mid-tones

contour

To make it simple to understand how to apply your shades of shadow I divided the eyelid into three sections: highlight, midtone and contour. The graph above will help you.

HIGHLIGHT

Your highlight shade is the lightest of the three eyeshadows. It can be dramatic or less dramatic, depending on the shade and the finish you select. A matte finish will give you a more subtle look than a shimmer finish. The shimmer will be more dramatic. For example, I usually use a shimmer highlight on deep-set eyes because it opens up the eye more than a matte shade. Also, the lighter the highlight shade, the more dramatic your look. A softer or flesh-toned shade will give you a less dramatic look. You should apply the highlight shade to your browbone and eyelid.

MIDTONE

Your midtone shade is your most important shade. It's the first step in the blending process and in creating the crease of the eye. This shade should be the most subtle – almost an extension of your skin. You'll change your highlight and contour colors more often than your midtone shade. Most of the time your midtone color should have a matte finish, but not always.

To apply it, start from the outside corner of the eyelid so that area will get the most midtone color. Gently move your brush across the crease into the inside corner of the eyelid. Depending on your eye shape, you may not always want to bring the color all the way over to the inside corner. Refer to Pages 116-129 for exact placement. If you want a very defined crease, you can apply a few more layers of your midtone shade, always making sure to blend it where it meets the highlight shade.

If you're short on time, just sweep your midtone color across your eyelids for a very natural look. It will help your eye color "pop," but won't help to define or shape your eyelids.

CONTOUR

The contour shade is the deepest of the three shades. It's not necessarily stark or dark -- it can even be metallic -- but it is the eyeshadow that is the deepest of the three. The contour eyeshadow is the shade you can have fun with and change with your mood. You'll find that most makeup lines offer more contour colors because they are the most eye-catching and exciting to use.

To apply, take a brush with shadow and move it across your top lashline from the outside corner, inward. Then bring the color up into the outer portion of the crease and blend it inward. This "layers" the contour shade on top of your midtone shade to help you get the blended, defined look you want. You can also apply the contour color underneath the lower lashline to define or blend it over your eye pencil.

For a more dramatic eye, you can always apply several layers of color to build the shade's intensity. Add color in small amounts. You can always add more for extra drama, but once you've applied it, it's difficult to remove. You can also do a smokey eye using your contour color over the entire lid, beginning at the lashline and blending it as you go upwards. For a true smokey look, you must blend, blend, and blend some more, otherwise your eyeshadow will appear too harsh.

Tip: You could also use a blush for your midtone if the product has been approved for the eye.

Tip: A quick note: the first place you lay your brush will receive the most color because it has the most product on it at the time.

Tip: Since blending is so vital to the overall effect of beautifully painted eyes, good quality shadow-brushes are a must because they enable you to create artful shapes and effects.

Tip: You should apply concealer or foundation to your lids first before applying eyeshadow. This helps the color blend more easily and wear longer.

pam frank

EYELINER

You can line and define your eyes in a number of ways: with pencil, liquid, cake, crème or powder. Or you can skip this step completely! It's a matter of personal choice.

PENCIL eyeliners contain silicone to help the color glide on smoothly and blend easily. Make sure the pencil you use doesn't have too much silicone, or the color will smear and smudge underneath your eyes rather than define them.

To apply pencil liner, begin at the outside corner of your eye and draw small, feather-like strokes, connecting each one as you move toward the inside of the eye, and then blend with a small brush. Using the same brush, apply a powder shadow in a similar color over the pencil to help make it look more natural. I always do this because it softens the pencil line and also sets the color. It also helps you correct any mistakes you may have made when blending the pencil strokes together.

For nighttime drama, I like to use a pencil underneath the eye and along the upper lashline. Make sure the line gradually grows thicker as it extends toward the outer corner of the eyes. Drawing the same thickness all the way across and underneath the eyelids can "close in" the eyes and make them appear smaller. For daytime, I normally don't use pencil underneath the eye. Instead, I like to use an eye shadow and a brush to create a softer, more natural look. If you prefer to wear pencil during the daytime, be sure to soften it by applying powder over it and make it appear more subtle.

Some women have a more noticeable rim of skin that is visible between the lashes and the eye, depending on their eye shape. You can darken this area with a pencil or a dark shadow to help your eye color "pop." One of my favorite tricks is to take black eyeshadow and carefully push it into the base of the lashes using a fine-tipped brush. This defines the eyes and makes the lashes look thicker without making your eyes appear "lined."

LIQUID eyeliner is the longest wearing and most brands come with a fine-tipped application brush. Liquid liner creates the strongest, most dramatic line. Never use liquid liner under the eye because it leaves an unnatural line that can be stark and hard-looking.

When using liquid eyeliner on the top of your eyelid, draw a continuous line starting at the inside corner to the outside corner of the eye, giving the line a little "kick" upwards at the end. Liquid eyeliner is the most difficult to apply, but you can master it with a little practice.

CRÈME eyeliner is also applied with a damp brush in the same manner as liquid and cake.

CAKE eyeliner comes as a powder. To apply, first dampen your brush then swipe it across the powder to form a liquid. Use the same method as liquid eyeliner to apply.

POWDER eyeliner, or eyeshadow used as liner, gives the most natural look and is the easiest to work with. You can use it dry or wet if you want a stronger look. To apply it dry, use a brush and draw a fine line along the base of the lashes from the outside to the inside corner of the eye. If you'd like to apply the powder wet, dampen your brush and apply it like liquid eyeliner. Powder used wet gives the same effect as liquid, but is much easier to control.

Tip: Always keep your pencils sharpened for more precise application.

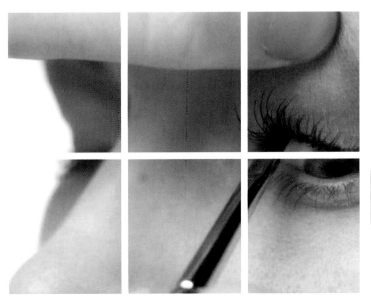

arlene lenarz

roshawnda r. foster

SKIN LEVEL: 11(bronze)
FACE SHAPE: heart-shaped face

SHADOWS: Highlight-shimmer gold
           Midtone-matte mahogany
           Contour-dark burgundy
OBJECTIVE: to create the illusion of a more oval-shaped face.
APPLICATION: contoured the temples and defined the hollows of the cheeks to help minimize the width of those area. Highlighted the chin to create the illusion of width. Highlighted the lid and browbone to open the eye. Used midtone shadow to even out her lids, then defined the lashline really well.

susan t. billy

SKIN LEVEL: 3 (fair)
FACE SHAPE: oval-shaped face
EYE SHAPE: hooded eyes
SHADOWS: Highlight-shimmer beige
           Midtone-matte taupe
           Contour-shimmer dark brown
OBJECTIVE: to contour the eyelid away to draw attention to the eyes.
APPLICATION: layered midtone and contour colors on hooded areas. The layering of color helps the end result appear more subtle and natural.

142

carol monteverde

144

wanda dalby

mary diamond

SKIN LEVEL: 4 (medium)
FACE SHAPE: round-shaped face
EYE SHAPE: hooded eye
SHADOWS: Highlight-shimmer flesh
　　　　　Midtone-matte taupe/ matte dark taupe
　　　　　Contour-shimmer golden brown
OBJECTIVE: to give the illusion of a more oval-shaped face. To minimize the hooded area and "open up" the eye.
APPLICATION: softly sculpted cheeks, jaw and temples to create a more oval shape. Applied midtone and contour

color to the hooded area of the lid to help them recede and "open up" the eye. Subtle layering of color creates a very natural effect. Then a really well defined lashline makes the blue in her eyes stand out.

145

julie baker

SKIN LEVEL: 5 (medium)
FACE SHAPE: square-shaped face
EYE SHAPE: hooded eyes
SHADOWS: Highlight-shimmer beige
　　　　　Midtone-matte taupe
　　　　　Contour-matte mahogany
OBJECTIVE: to give the illusion of a more oval-shaped face. To minimize the hooded appearance of her eyelids, making her eyes to appear more open and alive.
APPLICATION: contoured the hairline and jaw to soften the

"four corners". Highlighted down the center of the forehead, nose and the tip of the chin. Using midtone and contour colors, I applied, then blended them to the hooded area. This gave the illusion that the hooded area has receded.

susan porter glassmoyer

SKIN LEVEL: 5 (medium)
FACE SHAPE: oval-shaped face
EYE SHAPE: hooded eyes
SHADOWS: Highlight-shimmer beige
        Midtone-matte taupe
        Contour-shimmer golden brown
OBJECTIVE: to contour the lid away to draw attention to her eyes.
APPLICATION: layered midtone and contour colors on hooded areas. The layering of color helps the end result appear more subtle and natural.

lynda keene

SKIN LEVEL: 4 (medium)
FACE SHAPE: oval-shaped face
EYE SHAPE: wide-set eyes
SHADOWS: Highlight-shimmer beige
        M dtone-matte rose
        Contour-matte dark brown
OBJECTIVE: to visually bring the eyes closer together and to give her a youthful glow.
APPLICATION: layered the color in the crease and on the inside hollows of the eyes to visually pull the eye shape closer together. Used warm lip and cheek shades to give her skin a more youthful glow.

sonia paez

jan harris

dr. fran kaiser

SKIN LEVEL: 3 (fair)
FACE SHAPE: square-shaped face

SHADOWS: Highlight-shimmer flesh
              Midtone-matte taupe
              Contour-shimmer golden brown

OBJECTIVE: to create the illusion of a more oval-shaped face and to give her skin a more youthful glow.

APPLICATION: contoured the hairline and jaw to soften the "four corners." Highlighted the center of the forehead, nose, and tip of the chin. Highlighted the lid and browbone to open up the eye. Defined the crease and lashline to give the eye more shape. Chose a soft, warm blush to give her face a warm glow.

nancy castro

SKIN LEVEL: 6 (medium)
FACE SHAPE: square-shaped face

SHADOWS: Highlight-shimmer beige
              Midtone-matte taupe
              Contour-matte dark brown

OBJECTIVE: to create the illusion of a more oval-shaped face and to make her eye color "pop."

APPLICATION: contoured the hairline and jaw to soften the "four corners." Highlighted the center of the forehead, nose, and tip of the chin. Highlighted the lid and browbone to open up the eye. Defined the crease and lashline to give the eye more shape and to make eye color "pop."

jennifer stephens

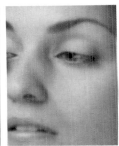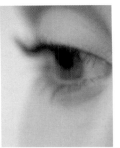

long lashes

I always recommend curling your eyelashes because it opens up the eyes and makes them appear larger and more youthful. Many women skip this step and it's a mistake. You're never too old to curl your lashes. But make sure the tool you use is young. If you use an eyelash curler for more than a year, it can get out of alignment and cut your lashes.

The trick to curling your eyelashes correctly is to crimp them more than just once at the lashline. Instead, "walk" the eyelash curler up the length of your lashes, taking care to close, open and move the eyelash curler up several times until you reach the end of your lashes. This method creates a curve rather than a crimp, and will help your eyelashes stay curled.

You can make your lashes look longer or thicker depending on how you apply your mascara. Thickening and lengthening mascaras contain particles that attach to the lash so you can control how you want to build your lashes.

For thicker lashes: start at the base of the lashes and hold your mascara wand in a horizontal position, working it from side to side as you work your way up to the end of the lashes. This makes the mascara particles attach to the sides of your lashes, making them appear thicker.

For longer lashes: Hold your mascara wand in a vertical position. Starting at the base of the lashline, pull the wand up and out to the end of your lashes. The particles will attach to the ends of your lashes, making them appear longer. Just make sure to choose the correct formula for your desired effect. If you want to define your lashes, use a defining formula. If you want to thicken, use a thickening formula. Turn to Page 33 for more information on the different mascara formulas that are available.

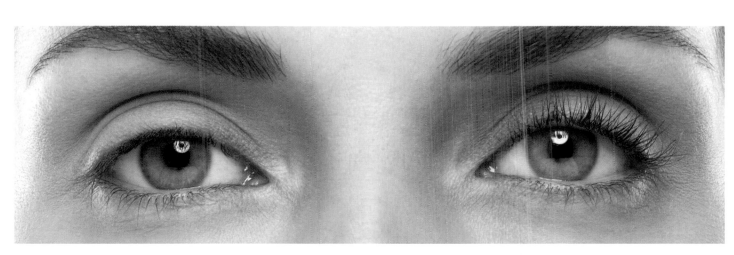

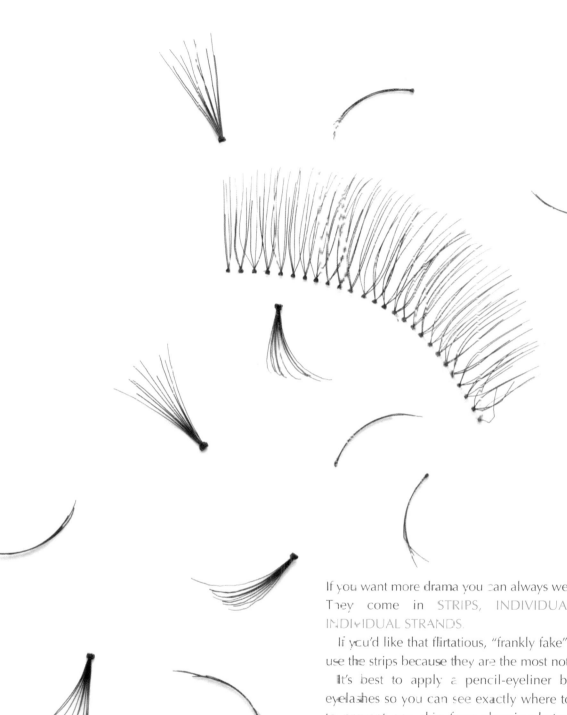

If you want more drama you can always wear false eyelashes. They come in STRIPS, INDIVIDUAL FLARES and INDIVIDUAL STRANDS.

If you'd like that flirtatious, "frankly fake" look for evening, use the strips because they are the most noticeable.

It's best to apply a pencil-eyeliner before your strip-eyelashes so you can see exactly where to place them and to prevent any skin from showing between your natural lashes and the false ones. The closer you place them to your natural lashline, the more natural they'll appear. You can follow with a liquid liner to help disguise the lash band.

The flares are more natural-looking than strips, but my preference is for the individual-strand lashes. They look the most natural, and they are the ones typically used for most mascara advertisements. You simply apply them directly on top of your own lashes to help extend the length.

Tip: I personally prefer to use black mascara on the upper lashes but brown on the lower ones because brown looks less harsh.

Tip: Make certain you coat the lashes at the inside corners and the very outer corners. These are the ones many women miss.

Tip: Two or three thinly applied coats of mascara are far more effective than a single, "clumpy" one.

erica tracy

SKIN LEVEL: 4 (medium)
FACE SHAPE: square-shaped face

SHADOWS: Highlight-shimmer beige
             Midtone-matte taupe
             Contour-shimmer golden brown
OBJECTIVE: to give the illusion of a more oval-shaped face.
APPLICATION: contoured hairline and jaw to soften the "four corners" of the face. Highlighted down the center of the forehead, nose, and the tip of the chin. Made sure to highlight the lid and brow bone to open the eye. Defined the crease and lashline to give the eye more shape.

allison piro

SKIN LEVEL: 3 (fair)
FACE SHAPE: heart-shaped face

SHADOWS: Highlight-shimmer flesh
             Midtone-matte taupe
             Contour-shimmer golden brown
OBJECTIVE: to give the illusion of a more oval-shaped face.
APPLICATION: contoured her temples and the hollows of her cheeks to minimize the width. Highlighted the chin to create the illusion of more width. Made sure to define the lashline really well to intensify the color of the eyes.

joanna hathcock

SKIN LEVEL: 4 (medium)
FACE SHAPE: square-shaped face

SHADOWS: Highlight-shimmer beige
Midtone-matte taupe
Contour-shimmer golden brown

OBJECTIVE: to create the illusion of a more oval-shaped face.

APPLICATION: contoured the hairline and jaw to soften the " four corners" of the face. Highlighted down the center of the forehead, nose and the tip of the chin to create an oval illusion. Joanna has very unusually shaped eyes, to accentuate them I really highlighted and contoured them Started by highlighting the lid and brow, then built contour color in the crease and at the lashline.

brooke tobolka

SKIN LEVEL: 5 (medium)
FACE SHAPE: square-shaped face

SHADOWS: Highlight-shimmer beige
Midtone-matte taupe
Contour-matte dark brown

OBJECTIVE: to create the illusion of a more oval-shaped face.

APPLICATION: contoured the hairline and jaw to soften the "four corners" of the face. Highlighted down the center of the forehead, nose and the tip of the chin. Brooke has slightly hooded lids so using midtone and contour colors, I applied, then blended them to this area to help them recede. Then I made sure to define the lashline really well.

cheekchic

Blush and bronzer work together to bring your face alive and give you a natural, healthy glow. Getting that beautiful glow is a two-step process because I always like to bronze the face before adding the actual cheek color. I think every woman can benefit from bronzing because it adds warmth and natural beauty to the skin, and can make you appear younger.

Before we learn how to bronze and blush correctly, I want to shatter the old myths of where and how to apply color to your cheeks.

Myth 1: Blush should never be worn closer to your nose than the width of two fingers. Depending on the width of your fingers, your blush could wind up on the side of your face instead of the apples of your cheeks!

Myth 2: Blush should never be applied below the tip of your nose. If you have a cute little turned up nose, your blush could be applied above the apples of your cheeks.

Myth 3: Apply blush as an inverted triangle to the face to give it more shape. We use foundation and powder to highlight and contour the face – not blush. Blush is used to add color and life to the skin.

Myth 4: Mature women should apply cheek color higher as they age. While the skin may lose some of its elasticity as we age, I can assure you that our cheekbones remain in the same place! If you know how to locate your cheekbones correctly, you'll always have your bronzer and blush in the right place on your face.

To accurately locate your cheekbones, take this can't-miss application test:

1. Smile.
2. Locate the center of the "apple" of your cheek and place your index finger there. Now place your thumb at the top of your ear where it connects to your head. Now take your thumb and bring it toward your index finger. The bone you feel is your cheekbone. Next, apply your color directly onto the cheekbone or slightly below it if you're trying to make it appear higher.

Tip: Keep a separate brush for bronzers and blush because it keeps each color clearer and purer.

BRONZER

Bronzer makes your skin look sun-kissed and alive. It gives your skin a healthy glow without subjecting it to damaging ultra-violet rays. To warm your face and accentuate your bone structure, simply dust bronzing powder or crème bronzer along the outer edges of your face and onto your cheekbones. Bronzer is also useful for lightly sculpting the nose and chin.

Always apply your bronzer beginning at the back of your cheekbone and sweep it forward. Then go back and brush in the opposite direction to blend. If you are using a crème bronzer, simply dot the color along your cheekbone and blend. Don't forget a little at the temples to help shape your face. Sweeping the bronzing powder up around the temples and the eye sockets can also really help your eye color pop, especially if your eyes are green or blue.

If bronzing powders and crèmes look too bold on you, try using pressed powder instead. It has a lower pigment level and blends very nicely. If you have lighter skin, an ebony pressed powder will work beautifully as a bronzer.

BLUSH

There are three major mistakes women make with blush.

1. Using too much of it in the fall and winter to try to compensate for the lack of a tan.

2. Choosing a color that is either too red or too purple. Remember, to help determine a good shade for yourself, try a short burst of energetic exercise then match your blush color to your cheeks' natural flush.

3. Applying too little of a shade because it's too strong, and therefore it doesn't last the day.

The intensity of color you are wearing on your eyes and lips can determine the amount of blush you might need that day. For example, if you are wearing a strong lip color, you will need less blush. If you are wearing a paler, sheerer lip color, you might need more blush. A powder blush is the easiest to use. There are two ways to apply your powder blush properly:

1. Apply blush to your cheekbone area, starting at the back closest to your ear. Sweep your cheek color toward the apple of your cheek then back toward the ear again. Then go back again in the opposite direction to blend. This way your most intense color lies at the back of your cheek and gives your face more dimension.

2. For a more natural appearance, you can try a technique called "popping your apples." First, apply bronzer to your cheekbones. Then take a light, sheer blush color, making sure it is not too dark. Smile and apply your blush color back toward the area that you bronzed. This gives the apples of your cheeks a beautiful glow. Again, you'll want to use a sheer shade of blush for this technique. A dark or bright cheek color can be too intense and unnatural looking.

If you use crème or liquid blush, apply it with either a sponge or your fingers after your foundation and before your powder for easier blending. If you wear your blush without foundation, crème and liquid work better than powder blush because they contain moisture that blends better with the natural moisture of your skin. To apply crème or liquid blush, first dot a little onto the apples of your cheeks and blend back toward your ears.

With any blush, you should remember the rule to match textures – crème on crème and powder on powder. To increase the staying power of your blush, try this tip:

1. Apply crème blush after you apply your foundation.

2. Apply your pressed or loose powder.

3. Apply powder blush on top of your face powder. It is the two layers of color that helps the cheek color stay on and last throughout the day.

> Tip: If cheek color is too intense, soften it with a dusting of loose powder.

> Tip: Never use blush to contour or shape the face.

ashley cantley

SKIN LEVEL: 4 (medium)
FACE SHAPE: pear-shaped face

SHADOWS: Highlight-shimmer beige
Midtone-matte taupe
Contour-shimmer golden brown
OBJECTIVE: to give the illusion of a more oval-shaped face.
Draw more attention to the eyes.
APPLICATION: contoured the jawline and the hollows of
the cheek to help minimize their width. Highlighted the
center of the forehead to help create width. To help bring
attention to the eyes, defined the lashline and the crease
really well.

holly jonsson

SKIN LEVEL: 3 (fair)
FACE SHAPE: square-shaped face

SHADOWS: Highlight-shimmer flesh
Midtone-matte taupe
Contour-matte dark taupe
OBJECTIVE: to give the illusion of a more oval-shaped face.
To define the features without the use of a lot of color.
APPLICATION: contoured the hairline and jaw to soften the
"four corners". Highlighted down the center of the forehead,
nose and the tip of the chin. I wanted a minimal look so I
used much more subtle colors to define with, therefore
giving you a practically no-makeup look.

patricia young

sidney helou

SKIN LEVEL: 8 (olive)
FACE SHAPE: square-shaped face

SHADOWS: Highlight-shimmer beige
Midtone-matte taupe
Contour-shimmer golden brown
OBJECTIVE: to give the illusion of a more oval-shaped face.
To subtly define her features.
APPLICATION: her skin is so amazing that I certainly did not have to do much. Contoured hairline and jaw to soften the "four corners" of the face. Highlighted down the center of the forehead, nose and tip of the chin. Highlighted her lids and browbones. Subtly defined her crease.

jordan helou

SKIN LEVEL: 6 (medium)
FACE SHAPE: square-shaped face

SHADOWS: Highlight-shimmer beige
Midtone-matte taupe
Contour-shimmer golden brown
OBJECTIVE: to give the illusion of a more oval-shaped face.
To subtly define her features.
APPLICATION: contoured hairline and jaw to soften the "four corners" of the face. Highlighted down the center of the forehead, nose and tip of the chin. Highlighted lids and brow bones then defined eyes at lashline and in the crease. Finished with glossy lips.

kathy helou

lips

To keep your lips looking luscious, exfoliate them once a week. I always like to use a little lip balm or moisturizer on the lips before I apply the lipstick color because it helps the lip liner and lipstick go on smoothly and more evenly. Just apply the lip balm first and blot off the excess.

Lip pencils will help prevent lipstick from feathering and bleeding, but once you've outlined your lips, don't stop there. Be sure to blend inward so that when your lipstick wears off you aren't left with just an outline. You'll find a brush useful in the application and blending.

Make sure you optimize your entire mouth. Most women don't because they tend to draw inside the lip line. Conversely, take care not to overdraw because if you're using a lip color other than a natural lip-tone and you stray too far outside the lip line, it will be noticeable.

BASIC

I'm often asked if women have to wear lip liner. While it's an optional step, here are three things to consider to help you decide if lip liner is for you:

1. Lip liner can help define your mouth and reshape your lips if they are uneven.

2. Lip liner can help prevent your lip color from bleeding onto your skin.

3. Lip liner can help your lipstick last longer, especially if you fill in your lips with liner first before applying your lip color.

To properly apply your lip liner to the top lip, begin with a V in the "cupid's bow" or center curve area of the lip. Then starting at the outer corners, draw small, feathery strokes to meet the center V.

On the lower lip, first accentuate the lower curve of the lip, then begin small feather-like strokes from the outer corners moving towards the center.

Now you can actually apply your color.

You can use a brush, your fingers or a tube to apply your lipstick, but if it's applied with a brush it will usually look much more precise and last longer. For more intense color you can apply it straight from the tube, but it will be harder to cover the smaller detailed areas of the lips.

TIP: Putting on lipstick straight from the tube will not blend your lip liner. You should always blend the liner with a brush toward the center of the lips.

Tip: Don't forget that brighter, warmer colors also make you look younger. Anything too dark is far too harsh for mature lips.

Tip: Remember that paler colors illuminate and make lips appear fuller and more youthful, while dark colors have a minimizing effect, making lips appear smaller.

braden harris

vanessa shasteen

SKIN LEVEL: 4 (medium)
FACE SHAPE: pear-shaped face
SHADOWS: Highlight-shimmer flesh
               Midtone-matte taupe
               Contour-matte dark taupe

OBJECTIVE: to give the illusion of a more oval-shaped face. To subtly define her features without making her look to mature.

APPLICATION: contoured the jawline and cheeks to help minimize their width. Highlighted the center of the forehead to create the illusion of more width. Subtly defined the eyes at the lashline and glossed the lips to give her a fresh young look.

167

tess mullen

SKIN LEVEL: 4 (medium)
FACE SHAPE: oval-shaped face
SHADOWS: Highlight-shimmer beige
               Midtone-matte taupe
               Contour-matte dark taupe

OBJECTIVE: to softly define the features and give her a polished sophisticated look.

APPLICATION: with an oval shaped face there was not a lot for me to do. Wanted to warm up the skin, so applied bronze. Next, subtly defined the eyes by highlighting the lids and brow bone. Then softly defined the crease and lashline with soft colors.

stefanie cox

SKIN LEVEL: 6 (olive)
FACE SHAPE: square-shaped face
EYE SHAPE: wide-set eyes
SHADOWS: Highlight-shimmer beige
          Midtone-matte taupe
          Contour-matte dark brown
OBJECTIVE: to give the illusion of a more oval-shaped face.
To help it appear as if the eyes are closer together.
APPLICATION: contoured the hairline and jaw to soften the
" four corners" of the face. Highlighted down the center of
the forehead, nose and the tip of the chin.
Layered midtone color in the crease and
on the inside hollow of the eyes to visually
pull the eye placement closer together.

sarah bird

SKIN LEVEL: 5 (medium)
FACE SHAPE: pear-shaped face

SHADOWS: Highlight-shimmer beige
          Midtone-matte taupe
          Contour-matte dark taupe
OBJECTIVE: to give the illusion of a more oval-shaped face. To
subtly define her features without making her look too mature.
APPLICATION: contoured the jawline and cheeks to help
minimize their width. Highlighted the forehead to create
the illusion of more width. Next, subtly
defined her eyes at the lashline and
highlighted her lids and brow bones.

stacy james

170

julianne

poppi monroe

SKIN LEVEL: 5 (medium)
FACE SHAPE: square-shaped face
SHADOWS: Highlight-shimmer flesh
             Midtone-matte taupe
             Contour-shimmer golden brown
OBJECTIVE: to create the illusion of a more oval-shaped face and to subtly define her features.
APPLICATION: contoured the hairline and jaw to soften the "four corners." Highlighted the center of the forehead, nose, and tip of the chin. Highlighted the lid and browbone to open up the eye. Defined the crease and lashline to give the eye more shape.

amy williams

SKIN LEVEL: 6 (medium)
FACE SHAPE: square-shaped face
SHADOWS: Highlight-shimmer beige
             Midtone-matte taupe
             Contour-matte dark brown
OBJECTIVE: to create the illusion of a more oval-shaped face and to bring out her eye color and draw attention to her eyes.
APPLICATION: contoured the hairline and jaw to soften the "four corners." Highlighted the center of the forehead, nose, and tip of the chin. Highlighted the lid and browbone to open up the eye. Defined the crease and lashline to give the eye more shape and to make eye color "pop."

SMALL LIPS

If you feel you have small lips, there are two ways to create a new, fuller lip look:

1. First, erase your existing lip line with concealer or foundation. Doing this creates a fresh canvas on which you can design a whole new and improved lip line.

2. Using natural-toned lip pencil, draw a line just slightly above your natural lip line on the top lip and around the bottom. Don't exaggerate the line – just slightly above and below your natural lip line is your goal.

3. Now fill in your lips with the lip liner completely, except for the very center of your top lip and bottom lip.

4. Take a dab of light concealer and place it in the center of your top lip and bottom lip. When you apply your lipstick, this area will remain lighter and help make your lips appear fuller.

5. To finish, apply a light, shimmery lip gloss to the center of your lips over your lipstick to help make your lips appear even fuller.

The second way to create fuller lips is by using two complementary shades of lip color – one lighter, one darker. First, line your lips with a natural-toned lip pencil. Then apply the darker shade of lip color on the outer edges of your lips, blending it where it meets the lip liner. Next, apply the lighter shade of lipstick on the inside of your lips and blend it where it meets the darker shade. Finally, take a light, shimmery lip gloss and place it in the center of the lips to create the illusion of fuller lips.

Choosing the correct formula for the desired lip look is important. Glossy is always sexy. The shine makes your lips appear fuller and more youthful. If your lips tend to be dry, stay away from matte lipstick. While the formula wears longer, it can make your lips look and feel even more dehydrated. Crème formulas are always a safe choice because they tend to work in just about any situation.

Play with lip color. Don't be afraid of it. It's always easy to change it. Just remember it's important to consider your lip size when choosing a lipstick color. Darker shades make the lips look smaller. Lighter shades make the lips look fuller. To review the guidelines for choosing lip color, turn to Pages 66 and 67.

One last point to remember: never expect lipstick to last all day. Formulas that do make the lips look parched and dry. These products contain stains that, unless your lips are freshly exfoliated, will adhere unevenly to the dry areas of your lips, causing your lipstick to appear splotchy and dehydrated.

Tip: Always moisturize your lips before applying color.

Tip: To help lipstick stay on longer, use lip liner all over your lips, apply lipstick on top, then blot and reapply.

Tip: To set your lipstick, try placing a single-ply tissue across your lips then lightly dust over it with a little loose powder.

debi moore

summary

Throughout the years I have been surrounded by beautiful, strong women, all of whom have greatly influenced my ideals of beauty.

My training in beauty began with many years of studying art, which I think is why I pay particular attention to the importance of shading, undertones and blending. My maternal grandfather was a talented artist and painter, so when my mother noticed very early on that I exhibited a similar gift I was encouraged to begin studying. As early as the sixth grade I won a scholarship to study painting and sculpture at the Museum of Fine Arts in Houston, Texas.

After many years of studying painting I grew tired of it, so I decided to focus my energy on acting. I then attended a high school for the performing arts and majored in theatre. That's where my interest in makeup really began, because along with performing in the productions I was encouraged to do the makeup for them. Actually it is there that I received my strongest encouragement to pursue my God-given talents in beauty. I then continued my education by studying all aspects of beauty, including hair and skin.

For as long as I can remember I have always been mesmerized by glamour. Like a lot of people of my generation, from a very early age I considered "Barbie" to be the absolute epitome of beauty and glamour. I have three sisters, and growing up we spent hours playing "Barbie". As far as we were concerned she had it all---beauty and brains.

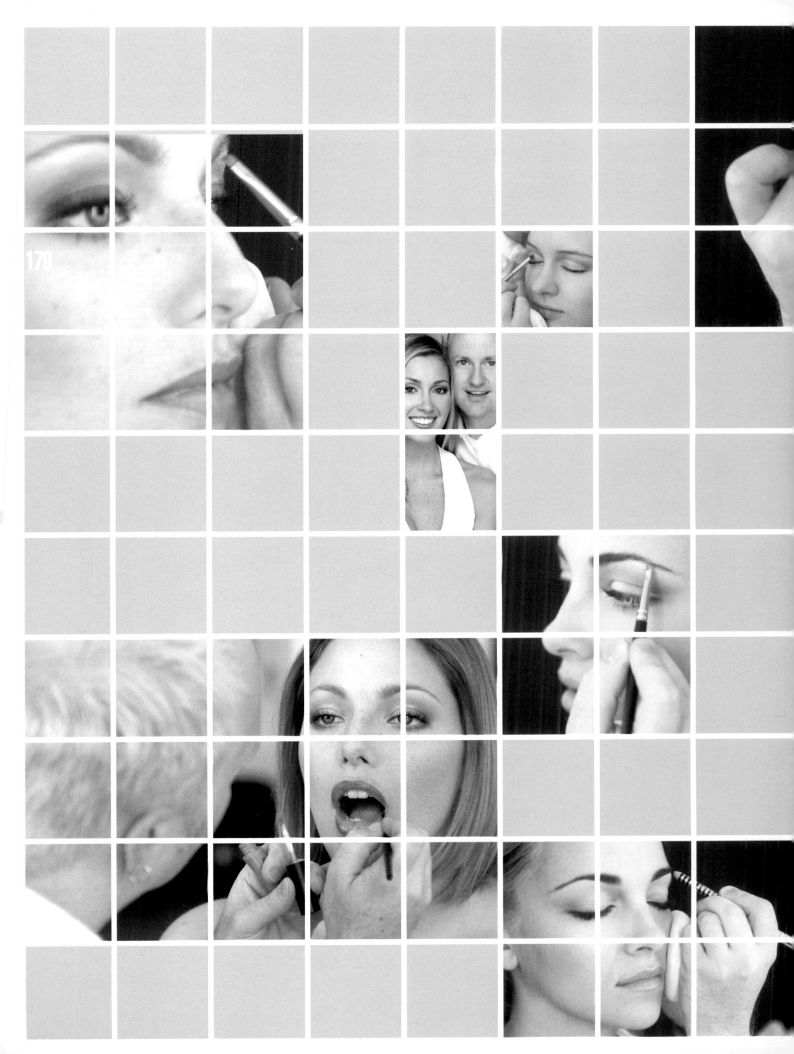

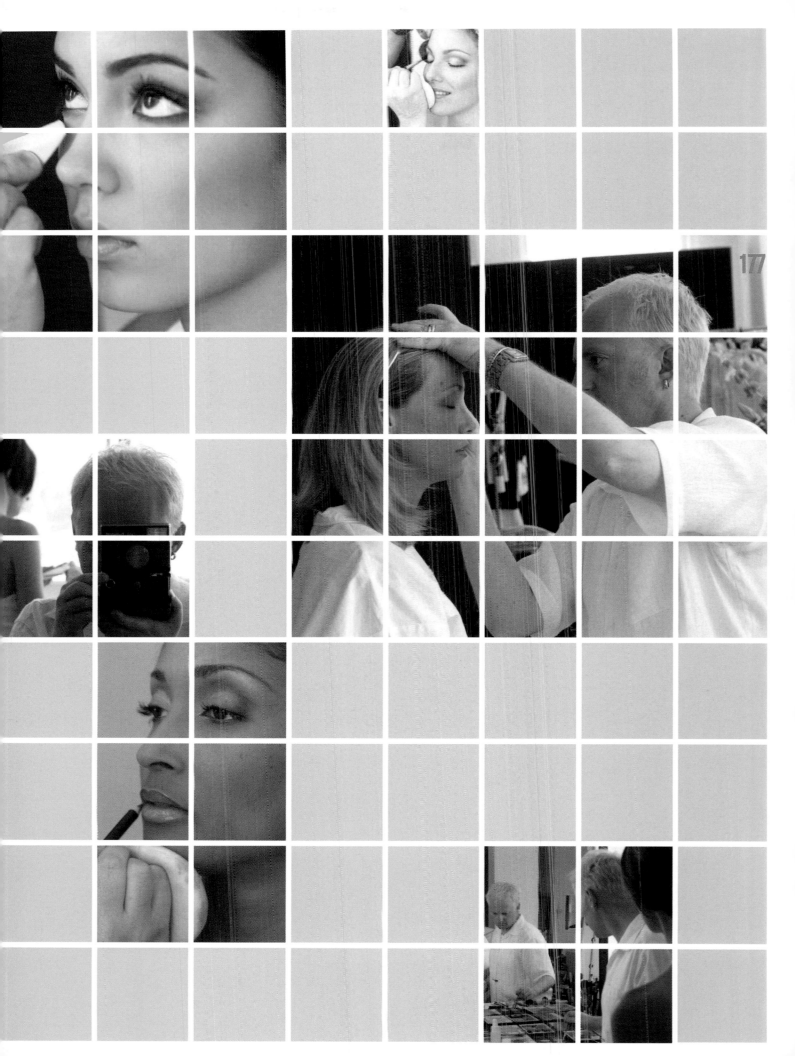

Growing up, it was "just me and five women". Along with my sisters there was my mom, who was single, and my grandmother, who was devoted to us. They each had their own style and weren't afraid to express it. I remember from a very young age begging my mother to grow her hair long and to wear dresses. I guess you could say I was destined for the fashion and beauty business. I remember going (sometimes once a week) with my mother and grandmother to the beauty shop, watching them get their hair done, and loving the experience.

One of my fondest childhood memories is of standing watching my grandmother with vast interest as she applied her make-up. Her eyebrows were always a little too dark and slightly crooked. I remember rosy-pink overdone cheeks and frosted, "cotton candy" pink lipstick. Nonna wore her makeup faithfully every single day. In fact I never saw her go anywhere without it on.

Another fond memory is of my mother as she prepared for a date in the very early 70's. It was becoming the latest thing to use mascara on the bottom lashes, and I remember sitting watching her and her look of concentration as she carefully applied it for the very first time. When she finished she turned to me and announced she felt that she looked a bit like Raggedy-Ann. Of course, I thought she looked fabulous.

Then there were my sisters. Occasionally, as we got older, I was able to practice hair and makeup on them. It didn't happen that often when we were young because my mother thought boys should not play with hair or paint faces. I still remember getting my younger sisters (who are twins) ready for their prom. I started with helping them shop for their dresses and finished by doing their hair and makeup for that special night. I guess I have always loved the transformation process.

Everything you have read here is subjective---these are my personal opinions on beauty.

Since education and knowledge is strength, I can only hope that the information compiled in my book will encourage you, boost your self-confidence and help you to reveal your true beauty.

As we end our time together, I want to leave you with this thought. Beauty isn't just about makeup. It's about self-confidence, individuality and the desire to embrace your inner beauty. These are the beauty marks that really make you unforgettable. Wear them proudly every day along with a smile and your own sense of style. And you'll be absolutely beautiful. Inside and out.

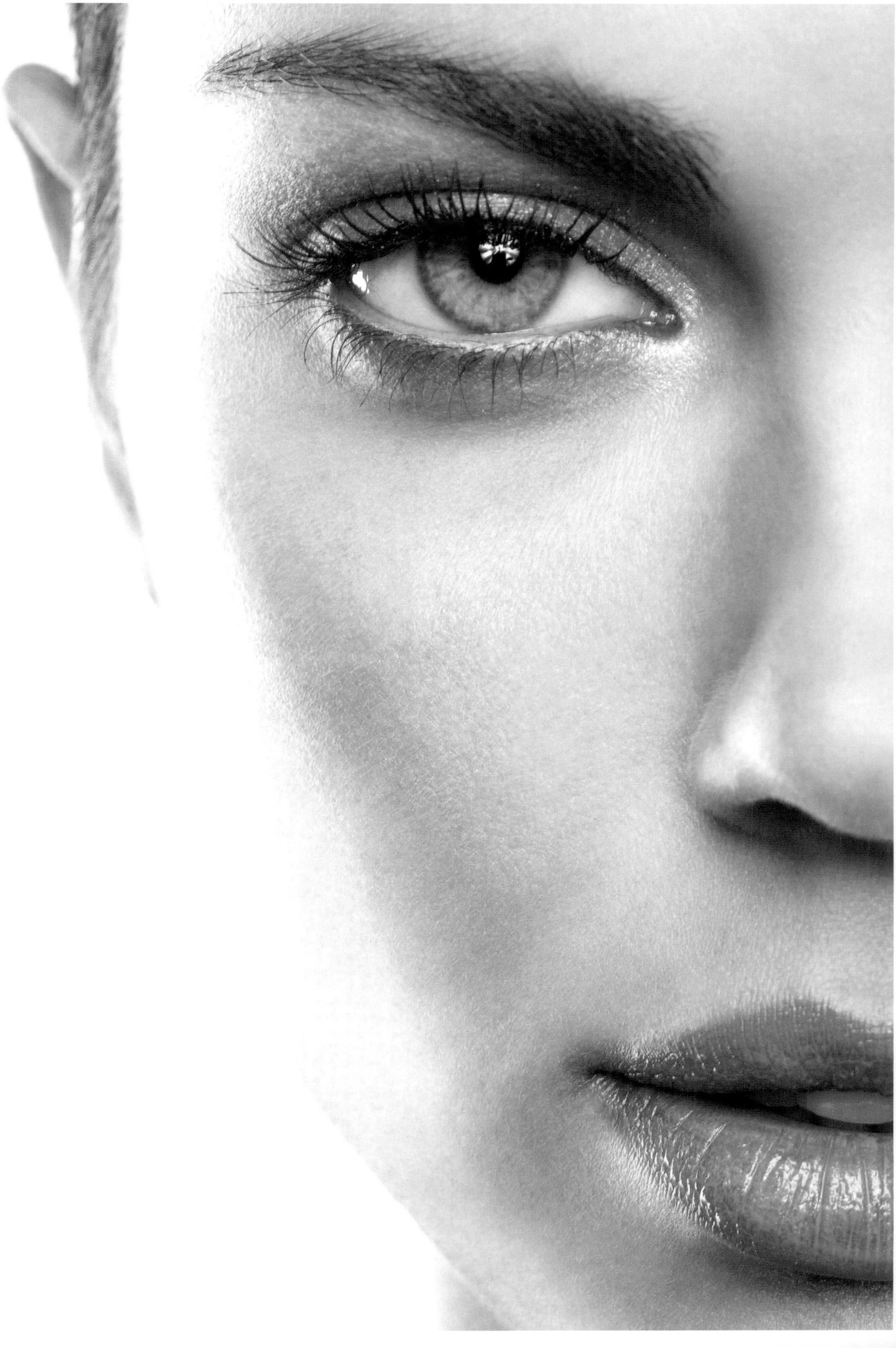

self confidence is the most important element of true beauty.
—robert jones